Twayne's United States Authors Series

Sylvia E. Bowman, *Editor*

INDIANA UNIVERSITY

Thornton Wilder

THORNTON WILDER

by REX BURBANK

San Jose State College

 5

Twayne Publishers, Inc.   ::   New York

To My Father
and
For My Wife

Preface

CRITICAL and popular recognition came suddenly to Thornton Wilder with the publication in 1927 of *The Bridge of San Luis Rey*, which became a best-seller almost immediately after it appeared. In its first year it had thirteen printings in England and sales of over a hundred thousand copies in the United States; it won Wilder the Pulitzer Prize for 1928. Success of *The Bridge* with both the public and the critics is not hard to account for: It represented a radical change from the realism that characterized the fiction of the twenties. As Harry Salpeter wrote in *Outlook* in 1928, readers of fiction "were tired of realistic novels and were rotten ripe for a book like *The Bridge*, whether they knew it or not."[1]

A good many critics also felt, like St. John Adcock, that the book was a welcome departure from the "naive school" of realism that dwelt inordinately upon the grosser aspects of life. *The Bridge*, Adcock declared with approval, portrayed "those equally real human qualities that help distinguish man from four-legged animals" and restored that "sense of mystery of life" lacking in the realistic fiction of the day.[2] Critics admired its stylistic clarity and gentleness of tone as well as its non-realistic matter. Arnold Bennett said in the London *Evening Standard* that he was "dazzled" by Wilder's performance and added: "The writing, simple, straight, just and powerful, has not been surpassed in the recent epoch."[3] And Alexander Woollcott, whose life-long admiration for Wilder began with *The Bridge*, described it as a "novel of aloof and untruckling beauty."[4]

The Bridge immediately put Wilder in the front rank of writers, and he enjoyed two years of widespread critical approval; even his first novel—*The Cabala*, published in 1926—received renewed attention and respect. But with the publication in 1930 of his third novel, *The Woman of Andros*, a critical reaction occurred: It was an unpropitious time for the appearance of a novel that took place in pre-Christian Greece and involved the melancholy longings of an Andrian hetaira for religious certitude. Wall Street had collapsed with the stock market crash in 1929, and lines of the unemployed were becoming appallingly long. As it became apparent that a full-scale depression was under way, the conviction grew among both critics and general readers that it was the responsibility of the writer to portray realistically and uncompromisingly the social problems of his country and his time.

While not everyone agreed with the Marxists that novelists should depict the class conflict—the struggle between the workers and the bosses—demand for a literature that was grounded in social realism was increasing. Remoteness of *The Woman of Andros* from the social problems of America, 1930, left Wilder vulnerable, therefore, to charges that he was either indifferent to them or unable to confront them. *The Cabala*, which took place in Rome, and *The Bridge*, whose action was set in seventeenth-century Peru, were only slightly less remote than *The Woman;* and the three-minute plays in *The Angel That Troubled the Waters* (1928), based in large part upon classical Greek and biblical myths, were even more removed. Works that only two years before had been timely departures from a too-realistic literary milieu were now considered superciliously indifferent to the real facts of life.

The first and most serious critical attack against Wilder in this period came on October 22, 1930, when the *New Republic* published an article by Michael Gold titled "Wilder: Prophet of the Genteel Christ." Gold accused Wilder of scornfully ignoring the social injustices in America and of writing for a "small sophisticated class." "Is Mr. Wilder a Swede or a Greek, or is he an American?" he demanded. "No stranger would know from the books he has written." He complained that Wilder "has all the virtues Veblen said this leisure class would demand: glossy high finish as against intrinsic qualities, conspicuous inutility, caste feeling, love of the archaic, etc. . . . This Emily Post of culture will never reproach them; or remind them of Pittsburgh or the breadlines." He charged that Wilder's religion "isn't the fervent religion of the Holy Rollers or Baptists or Tolstoy or Dostoyevsky. It is Anglo-Catholicism, that last refuge of the American snob . . . it is that newly fashionable literary religion that centers around Jesus Christ, the First British Gentleman."

Gold's attack set off a controversy that brought hundreds of letters to the *New Republic,* "some carefully reasoned, some violent, and almost hysterical," as Malcolm Cowley wrote later in *Exile's Return.* Generally, the weight of responsible criticism was on Wilder's side, for Henry Hazlitt defended him in *The Nation,*[5] Edmund Wilson in the *New Republic.*[6] And when the quarrel ended, it was evident—Cowley wrote in retrospect—that Gold had "ridiculously overstated his case; he had failed to see that Wilder was a serious writer preoccupied with moral problems and that they were our own problems, even though Wilder's characters were disguised in Peruvian or Greek Costumes. . . ."[7]

But while Wilder retained a large popular following and the approval of a good many able critics, the Gold dispute had the unhappy effect of making the critics cautious about showing enthusiasm for him. Many of them had been too profuse in their admiration of his "aesthetic" qualities; and, with the onset of the depression, they were not prepared to make a case for fiction that said nothing about slum conditions, unemployment, or absentee ownership. As a result, Wilder got little attention for the next eight years.

But then, with the success of *Our Town* in 1938 and *The Skin of Our Teeth* in 1942—for each won Wilder a Pulitzer Prize—the critical pattern of lavish praise followed by attack and, finally, neglect or indifference was repeated. Like *The Bridge, Our Town* and *The Skin of Our Teeth* were timely. *Our Town* was staged at a time when Americans were beginning to rediscover their democratic heritage after their disillusionment with the shabby materialism and the subsequent economic paralysis the nation had fallen into in the twenties and thirties. *The Skin of Our Teeth* appeared just after the outbreak of World War II, when disaster seemed imminent. Both plays were affirmative in spirit and were well received at least partly because they answered the need of the times for affirmation.

However, in 1942 another controversy, nearly as violent as the Gold dispute twelve years before, developed when Joseph Campbell and Henry Morton Robinson, then making their "key" to James Joyce's *Finnegans Wake,* discovered that Wilder had borrowed much of his material for *Skin* from the

Joyce novel. In a series of articles appearing in the *Saturday Review* under the title "The Skin of Whose Teeth?" Campbell and Robinson drew parallels between the two works in characters, structure, and style; and, in effect, they accused Wilder of plagiarism. Like Gold, they ridiculously overstated their case: They confused Wilder's indebtedness to Joyce with deceitful appropriation of Joyce's material; but the effect of their attack was the same as that of Gold's. When the controversy was over, critics, seemingly exhausted by the subject of Wilder, gave him scant attention for the next decade.

This peculiar critical history has resulted in a failure by critics to explore Wilder's art and, consequently, in the establishment of certain stock attitudes towards it. It has been fashionable in some quarters to regard him as a schoolbook author whose works have the kind of perspicuity, didacticism, and tearful optimism that makes them suitable for high-school anthologies but not material for critical analysis. Among a good many critics who ought to know better a belief has grown that because he has had popular success Wilder has sinned against their critical rule of thumb that an author cannot be good if he is popular. The assumptions behind these views have enough truth in them to be troublesome. Wilder's works—particularly *The Bridge, Our Town, The Matchmaker,* and "The Happy Journey"—do have the ingredients that appeal to young audiences and are widely read or enacted in the schools. Moreover, he does take a more optimistic attitude towards life than most of his contemporary writers. And he is undoubtedly one of the most popular writers of his day.

But there is more than enough in Wilder's novels and plays to engage the adult mind and to interest the reader or viewer who expects more from literary art than amusement. With Wilder now in his sixties, and much (though by no means all) of his work behind him, it is possible—through close study of his work—to clear away some of the critical platitudes that have obscured him, to measure his achievement against his total artistic intent, and to place him where he belongs in the American tradition. The purpose of this book is to achieve these ends.

REX BURBANK

San Jose State College

Acknowledgments

I am deeply grateful for the help I have had while writing this book. I wish to thank Miss Isabel Wilder, sister of Mr. Wilder, for her kindness and generosity in providing me with valuable information about her brother and about his work. I also want to thank Mr. Wilder himself for making available to me materials—including the as yet unpublished *The Alcestiad*—I could not otherwise have obtained. I am particularly indebted to Joe Lee Davis for his discerning criticism of my work and for his penetrating suggestions. To Kenneth Rowe, Carlton Wells, and Fred Walcott I am grateful for generous interest, perceptive comments, and suggestions. I have indeed been fortunate in the help I have received, but I myself am responsible for any errors in fact or faults in judgment.

I wish to make special acknowledgment for permission to quote from the following works still in copyright:

To Harper and Brothers for permission to quote from *Heaven's My Destination, Our Town, The Skin of Our Teeth, The Matchmaker,* and *The Ides of March* by Thornton Wilder; and from *Spiritual Problems in Contemporary Literature,* edited by Stanley Romaine Hopper.

To the *American Scholar* for permission to quote from "Thornton Wilder: 'The Notation of the Heart'" by Edmund Fuller, which appeared in the spring, 1959, issue.

To Harcourt, Brace and Company for the passage from *Selected Essays 1917-1932* by T. S. Eliot, copyright, 1932, by Harcourt, Brace and Company, Inc.; renewed, 1960, by T. S. Eliot. Reprinted by permission of the publishers.

To Holt, Rinehart and Winston, Inc. for permission to quote from John Gassner's *Form and Idea in Modern Theatre* and from Paul Cubeta's *Modern Drama for Analysis.*

To The Viking Press, Inc. for permission to quote from Malcolm Cowley's *Exile's Return.*

To Princeton University Press for permission to quote from

Wilder's "Thoughts on Playwrighting," in *The Intent of the Artist*, edited by Augusto Centeno; and from Paul Elmer More's *On Being Human*.

To Albert and Charles Boni, Inc., Publishers, for permission to quote from *The Cabala, The Bridge of San Luis Rey*, and *The Woman of Andros* by Thornton Wilder.

To Coward-McCann, Inc. for permission to quote from *The Angel That Troubled the Waters, The Long Christmas Dinner and Other Plays* by Thornton Wilder.

To Longmans, Green and Co., Ltd. (London) for permission to quote from J. B. Coates' *The Crisis of the Human Person*.

To *The Saturday Review* for permission to quote from Ross Parmenter's "Novelist into Playwright," which appeared in the June, 1938, issue.

To Random House for permission to quote from Wilder's Introduction to *The Geographical History of America by Gertrude Stein*.

And to Mr. Thornton Wilder for permission to quote from "James Joyce (1882-1941)," which appeared in the March, 1941, issue of *Poetry: A Magazine of Verse*, and from *The Alcestiad*—as yet unpublished.

Contents

Chronology

1897 April 17, born in Madison, Wisconsin.

1905- Lived in Shanghai and Hong Kong during father's term
1909 as consul general.

1910- Resided in Berkeley, California. First efforts at writing.
1912

1913 Graduated from Thacher School, Ojai, California.

1915 First three-minute plays in *The Angel That Troubled the Waters,* written in Berkeley.

1915- Attended Oberlin College, studying classics under Professor Charles Wager.
1917

1917- At Yale to continue undergraduate study.
1918

1918- Served in Coast Artillery.
1919

1919- Back at Yale, working on the *Yale Literary Magazine* and writing one-act plays.
1920

1919- October to January, first full-length play, *The Trumpet Shall Sound,* published serially in the *YLM.*
1920

1920 Took A.B. at Yale. Left for Europe.

1920- Studied archaeology at American Academy in Rome. Impressions later recorded in *The Cabala.*
1921

1921 Accepted teaching job at Lawrenceville School.

1924 Published "A Diary: First and Last Entry" (short story) in *S4N.*

1926 *The Cabala* published.

1927 *The Bridge of San Luis Rey* published.

1928   *The Angel That Troubled the Waters* published.

1928   First Pulitzer Prize—for *The Bridge*.

1928- Resigned from Lawrenceville, toured Europe with
1930   sister Isabel, studied Continental theatre.

1930   *The Woman of Andros* published.

1931   *The Long Christmas Dinner and Other Plays* published.
      Accepted Robert Hutchins' invitation to lecture at the
      University of Chicago.

1933   Translation of Obey's non-realistic *Lucrece* published.

1935   Invited Gertrude Stein to lecture at Chicago.
      Heaven's My Destination published.

1936   Left University of Chicago. Began career as serious
      dramatist.

1938   January 22, *Our Town* first performed, Princeton, New
      Jersey.
      December 12, *The Merchant of Yonkers* first produced,
      Boston.
      Awarded Pulitzer Prize for *Our Town*.

1941   One-year lectureship at Chicago.
      Lectures on James Joyce. At work on *Skin of Our Teeth*.

1942   October 15, *The Skin of Our Teeth* first performed,
      New Haven.
      Enlisted in U.S. Air Force in May, serving in U.S.A.,
      North Africa, and Italy until September 9, 1945.

1943   Third Pulitzer Prize, for *Skin of Our Teeth*.

1948   Translated Sartre's *Morts sans sepulture* (*The Victors*)
      for American stage.
      The Ides of March published.

1949   Lecture at Goethe Festival, Aspen, Colorado.

1950- Charles Eliot Norton Lectures at Harvard on Thoreau,
1951   Melville, and Emily Dickinson.

1952   Awarded Gold Medal for Fiction by Academy of Arts
      and Letters.

1954   August, *The Matchmaker* performed at Edinburgh Festival.

1955   August, *A Life in the Sun* (*The Alcestiad*) performed at Edinburgh Festival.

1955-   Work in Progress: Two opera librettos, cycle of one-act
1961   plays on the seven ages of man.

Thornton Wilder

CHAPTER 1

Early Expressions of Humanism

THREE FACTORS in Thornton Wilder's early life have had continued influence upon his work: a religious family background, an education which emphasized the classical works of literature, and widespread travel. Wilder was born on April 17, 1897, in Madison, Wisconsin, where his father owned and edited a newspaper. His father, Amos P. Wilder, was a devout Congregationalist; his mother, Isabel Niven Wilder, was the daughter of the Reverend Doctor Niven, pastor of the Presbyterian Church of Dobbs Ferry, New York.

After receiving his doctorate in economics at Yale, Amos Wilder entered newspaper work in New Haven where he edited first the *Palladium* and then the *Journal* before moving to Madison. An active supporter of Theodore Roosevelt, he was appointed consul general to Shanghai and Hong Kong during the second Roosevelt administration. When his tour of duty ended, he brought his family to California, where they resided in Berkeley and Ojai.

Thornton attended the missionary school in Chefoo, China, while the family was there but finished high school in California. After graduation, he and his brother, Amos Niven, were sent to college; they became, respectively, a teacher and a theologian. Amos N. Wilder, now a professor of theology at Harvard, has written widely about the spiritual aspects of contemporary literature. Thornton started his college training at Oberlin College in Ohio, interrupted his studies in 1917 for a year's service in the Coast Artillery, and then finished his undergraduate work at Yale where he received his degree in 1920. After spending 1920-21 in Rome studying archaeology at the American Academy, he returned to the

United States in 1922 to begin his teaching career at the
Lawrenceville boys' preparatory school near Princeton, New
Jersey, where he taught for six years. Success of *The Bridge
of San Luis Rey* in 1928 enabled him to resign and to devote
all his time to writing and traveling.

Recalling the differences between his contemporaries and
himself during the twenties, Wilder told a *Time* reporter in
1953: "I am the only American [writer] of my generation who
did not 'go to Paris.'"[1] While this is not literally true, it is
true in the sense that he did not go to Paris as a *déraciné*—a
voluntary exile from America. Unlike contemporaries such as
Hemingway and Glenway Wescott, Wilder did not feel nor
express in his work a nostalgia for or an isolation from a
locale in which he had lived or spent time during his childhood. He had never lived in one place long enough to grow
attached to it, and he seems to have felt at home wherever
he went. Nor did he break with the religious and moral traditions he had inherited from his parents, as did so many
young men and women of his time.[2] Moreover, his education,
leaning heavily towards the classics, abetted an admiration
for cultural tradition, a view of life that regarded its ethical
values as timeless and universal, and an attitude towards
literature that stressed its moral functions.

These factors are all mirrored in the religious, moral, and
aesthetic themes and, to a certain extent, in the style of the
three-minute plays in *The Angel That Troubled the Waters*.
Published in 1928, this volume includes sixteen of about forty
such plays Wilder wrote between 1915 and 1927. He stated
his intentions in the foreword to the book:

> I hope, through many mistakes, to discover the spirit that
> is not unequal to the elevation of the great religious themes,
> yet which does not fall into repellent didacticism. Didacticism
> is an attempt at the coercion of another's free mind, even
> though one knows that in these matters beyond logic, beauty
> is the only persuasion. Here the schoolmaster enters. . . .
> He sees all that is fairest in the Christian tradition made
> repugnant to the new generations by reason of the diction
> in which it is expressed. The intermittent sincerity of gener-
> ations of clergymen and teachers has rendered embarrassing
> and even ridiculous all the terms of the spiritual life. Nothing

succeeds in damping the aspirations of the young today—who dares use the word 'aspiration' without enclosing it, knowingly, in quotation marks?—like the names they hear given to them. The revival of religion is almost a matter of rhetoric. The work is difficult, perhaps impossible (perhaps all religions die out with the exhaustion of the language), but it at least reminds us that Our Lord asked us in His Work to be not only as gentle as doves, but as wise as serpents.

These plays—and most of his subsequent works—are attempts to bring fresh life and meaning to the "terms of the spiritual life." They are all parables or fables teaching Platonic or Christian lessons whose subjects include faith, love, humility, sacrifice, and the role and responsibility of the artist in society. The characters, for the most part one-dimensional, act upon one or another of these qualities—or upon superstition, reason, pride, or selfishness.

The first play in the volume, "Nascuntur Poetae," sets forth Wilder's Platonic theory of art. The Boy, who represents the unborn soul of the Poet, is shown being instructed in his responsibilities as an artist just prior to his birth into life from the world of eternal ideas. After being given the "gifts of pride and joy" by the Woman in the Chlamys, he is compelled by the Woman in Deep Red to accept "the dark and necessary gifts": a staff, for his journey through a life in which he will know no home; a crystal ball, which will enable him to see where other men cannot see, but which will forever deprive him of peace and satisfaction; and a chain, which will be a constant reminder of his obligations to his sacred calling and to his fellowmen. She says to him: "The life of man awaits you, the light laughter and the misery in the same day, in the selfsame hour the trivial and the divine. You are to give it voice. Among the bewildered and the stammering thousands you are to give it a voice and to mark its meaning."

This mystical, Platonic view of the writer and his purpose is found again in "Centaurs," where the romantic Shelley and the realist Ibsen are shown to have drawn the ideas for their works from the same transcendent source of eternal ideas, even though they used different forms and modes of presentation. Shelley expresses Wilder's conviction that "the stuff of

which masterpieces are made drifts about the world waiting
to be clothed in words. It is a truth that Plato would have
understood that the mere language, the words of a masterpiece are the least of its offerings."

Platonism takes on a Christian cast in "Mozart and the
Gray Steward." In this play, the Gray Steward (Death),
assuming the role of an emissary from a nobleman, arrogantly
offers Mozart a commission to write a requiem mass for the
nobleman's deceased wife. Mozart refuses, declaring that the
nobleman and his wife are unworthy of his music. The Gray
Steward then reveals his true self and accuses Mozart of failing in his obligation to "give a voice to all those millions
sleeping, who have no one but you to speak for them." "Only
through the intercession of great love," he tells Mozart, "and
of great art which is love, can that despairing cry be eased."
Christian humility becomes a moral responsibility for the
artist when the Gray Steward, identifying the kingdom of art
with the kingdom of heaven, warns Mozart that "only he who
has kissed the leper can enter the kingdom of art."

Platonic and Christian mysticism conjoin in "And the Sea
Shall Give up Its Dead," "Leviathan," and "Child Roland to
the Dark Tower Came," in which the characters—dreading
more than anything else the loss of their individuality—cling
to their identity after death but lose all traces of self in the
mystical "blaze of unicity" that is at once the realm of eternal
ideas and the Mind of God. More directly and exclusively
Christian are "Now the Servant's Name Was Malchus" and
the last three plays in the volume, "Hast Thou Considered My
Servant Job?" "The Flight into Egypt," and "The Angel That
Troubled the Waters." These four plays have biblical characters and put forth Christian paradoxes.

In the first of these, the infinite mercy of Christ contends
with and prevails over Satan's knowledge of human nature
for the soul of the betrayer Judas. The title of this play is, of
course, ironic and serves to accentuate the infiniteness of
God's mercy through the contrast between the suffering
servant Job and the traitor Judas. The theme of "The Flight
into Egypt" is the discrepancy between faith and the facts of
life. Indirectly, it is a gently satiric warning to believers that
the attempt to rationalize faith is futile, that the real source

of their faith is revelation, and that the best way to "prove" their faith is to live it. The donkey Hepzibah, who carries the Virgin Mary and the infant Jesus into Egypt, is the believer who insists on discussing with Mary the "matter of faith and reason." As Hepzibah discusses the question, she slows her pace and thus endangers her riders who symbolize the revealed justification for faith. When it occurs to her whom she is carrying, she admits that "it's a queer world where the survival of the Lord is dependent on donkeys, but it is so," and is advised by Mary to "do as I do and bear your master on."

In "The Angel That Troubled the Waters," the paradox of power-in-suffering arises from an action in which a man, a newcomer among the world's sufferers, asks the Angel who relieves sufferers to cure him of the impurity of his heart and his feelings of guilt so he can give his life to "Love's service"; that is, in service to mankind. The Angel refuses, saying: "It is your very remorse that makes your low voice tremble into the hearts of men. The very angels themselves cannot persuade the wretched and blundering children on earth as can one human being broken on the wheels of living. In Love's service only the wounded soldiers can serve."

Variations on the theme of the suffering servant of God—the Job theme—appear frequently in later works and so do variations on the Kierkegaardian theme of the absurd which appears in "Now the Servant's Name Was Malchus." In this play Malchus asks Our Lord to erase his name from the Book because people on earth have come to think of him as ridiculous because he had lost an ear to the sword of St. Peter while in the service of the High Priest. God replies that He too is ridiculous: "My promises were so vast that I am either divine or ridiculous. Malchus, will you stay and be ridiculous with me?" Like "The Flight into Egypt," this play contains a reminder to the faithful not to put too literal a construction on the Bible.

Each of these four plays is the work of a believer speaking primarily to other believers and cautioning them against intolerance, against trying to justify faith with reason, and against biblical literalism. Didactic, but not offensively so, they recall that faith is very difficult to maintain in the face of reason and the unpleasant facts of life—and that it is more often accompanied by suffering and doubt than by comfort and certitude.

The very conventionalism of such themes puts considerable burden upon the writer's power to give them fresh expression; and Wilder's extensive use of characters and materials from the cultural past instead of from life compounds this problem. But effective use of expressionistic techniques and of irony gives most of these plays remarkable vigor and novelty. Short as they are, they do develop and resolve conflicts. They build their tension dialectically, for the characters who embody ideas are pitted against one another. Most of the plays have, therefore, two main characters and a minor one. Usually the two main characters are moral protagonists: one holds conventional or superficial notions about such moral virtues as love, humility, and responsibility, about the role of art and the artist in life, or about religious faith and death; and the other, the stronger one, contends against these with ideas less soothing to human wishes, less intolerant, or less easily acceptable in terms of human pride or reason.

In "Fanny Otcott," for instance, a Bishop, grown "respectable" but feeling remorseful about an early stage career and a love affair with actress Fanny Otcott, calls upon her to announce that he intends to make a public confession of his youthful sins in order to clear his conscience of its burden of guilt. Fanny—a woman of questionable virtue by his recently acquired conventional concept of propriety—angrily denounces the greater immorality of his narrow moral orthodoxy. "You have borrowed your ideas from those who have never begun to live and who dare not," she tells him. Dedicated to life and the celebration of it in art, she refuses to make the love affair of their youth an immoral thing. She dismisses the Bishop, who has become spiritually attenuated by the binding restrictions of his creed, with: "Go away and tell your congregations what you please. I feel as though you were communicating to my mind some of those pitiable remorses that have weakened you. I have sinned, but I do not have that year [of our love affair] on my conscience. It is that year and my playing of Faizella that will bring troops of angels to welcome me to Paradise. Go away and tell your congregations what you please."

Looking back upon an artistic apprenticeship served in the writing of these plays, Wilder wrote in the foreword to *The Angel*: "The training for literature must be acquired by the artist alone, through the passionate assimilation of a few masterpieces written from a spirit somewhat like his own, and of a few masterpieces written from a spirit not at all like his own. I read all Newman and then I read all Swift. The technical processes of literature should be acquired almost unconsciously on the tide of a great enthusiasm, even syntax; even sentence-struction; I should like to hope, even spelling."

The characters and materials of these plays indicate clearly enough what masterpieces he was passionately assimilating in his youth: the Bible, Plato, Greek and Roman myths, nineteenth-century dramas of Shelley and Ibsen. Noticeably lacking, therefore, are materials from literary works of this century. The technical aspects of the plays also signify an absence of influence by the realism, fostered in the late nineteenth century by Ibsen and Henri Becque, that prevailed in the early years of the twentieth century. Although Wilder's non-realism in these plays derives ultimately from the classical Greek stage, the most immediate technical influence upon him was the expressionism of Strindberg. Despite Wilder's assertion that the technical processes of literature should arise from the "tide of . . . great enthusiasm," his admiration for Strindberg's dramaturgy at this time seems to have been considerable: Props and characters representing and expressing ideas in their undisguised form remind one strongly of the expressionistic *A Dream Play* and *Ghost Sonata,* as do the stage directions which call for animated scenery.

At times, however, Wilder's non-realism, going beyond even Strindberg's, precludes any kind of enactment. This passage from "Hast Thou Considered My Servant Job?" for instance, could hardly be enacted: "Suddenly the thirty pieces of silver are cast upward from the revolted hand of Judas. They hurtle through the skies, flinging their enormous shadows across the stars and continue falling forever through the vast funnel of space." The only way to get the idea in the final clause across on stage would be to have it recited chorally, a narrative stage technique Wilder utilized extensively in such later plays as "Pullman Car Hiawatha," *Our Town,* and *The Alcestiad,* where a stage manager or another character addresses the audience directly about matters that cannot be satisfactorily expressed in action. There is, however, no chorus-person indicated for the three-minute plays and for that reason most of them could not be given full dramatic expression on stage. The problem of dramatizing abstractions and supernatural events without resorting to straight narrative was one that Wilder had to solve before he could satisfactorily stage the non-realistic play he wanted to do.

The hand of the novelist is clearly visible in the narrative passages, particularly in the stage directions, of these plays. But more apparent in the total impression they achieve is the apprentice poet. The style is, for the most part, formal, poetic, "elevated." Especially noticeable are the conceits that plague young writers; and, on occasion, the language becomes precious and affected where personifications and pathetic fallacies appear and when the subjunctive mode is used: "Even though all Versaille kill me with steel pins, Quinte shall have the watch" ("The Penny Beauty Spent"). Or when the present or perfect is used where a future tense might be less melodramatic: "It has broken my will. I am in flight for Padua. My family are become nothing but sparrows" ("The Message and Jehanne").

These affectations, along with the melodrama and sentimentality that accompany them, seldom occur in subsequent works in which Wilder's style takes on the idioms and rhythms of everyday language. But the plays manifest other stylistic traits that have stayed with him through the years, and one is the short sentence. From "Nascuntur Poetae": "I am not afraid of life. I will astonish it. Why are we delaying?" From "Brother Fire":

> ISOLA: I like to play with fire.
> ANNUNZIATA: What a thing to say!
> ISOLA: I like to let my hair into it, gently, gently, gently, gently.

This last sentence also illustrates another trait: repetition. The Woman in the Chlamys says to the Boy in "Nascuntur Poetae": "Be not so eager for life. Too soon you will be shaken by breath; too soon and too long you will be tossed about by the chain. Take back your gifts. Take back life." The repetition in these lines provides syntactical balance and parallelism which intensify and build a unit of dialogue to a climax. Wilder uses this device with considerable effect both here and in his later works to achieve a stylistic intensity that compensates for lack of dramatic conflict. It is particularly effective in conveying a sense of inner tension.

Another stylistic device of these plays which Wilder has used increasingly as his works have become more philosophical is the aphorism. Found, usually, in the lines of characters of authority or wisdom, it serves as a succinct theme-statement which follows or precedes dramatic illustration or spoken elaboration. In "Mozart," when the Gray Steward says, "Know henceforth that only he who has kissed the leper can enter the kingdom of art," he states the meaning of the action that has preceded the statement. In the hands of an unskilled writer, of course, the aphorism can lapse into banality and oversimplification; but Wilder generally avoids both pitfalls by means of an ironic discrepancy between what is expected and what is actually said—as in the above instance, where "art" is substituted for "heaven"—which turns a commonplace proverb into a fresh idea.

Three obvious but salient factors appear, therefore, from the examination of the themes, technique, and style of these plays. First, they are Christian—and more openly so than any of Wilder's subsequent works, except possibly *The Woman of Andros*. Secondly, they are humanistic; and, thirdly, they are technically and stylistically non-realistic. The directness with which Wilder presents his Christian mystical and moral themes gives way, however, in later works to a more indirect, ironic presentation in which they emerge from a humanistic foundation—from a vision of life that establishes individual moral conduct as the first and indispensable element in harmonious existence. But the general features of Wilder's humanism and its relationship to religious faith can be found in *The Angel* in his Platonism, his use of classical and biblical materials, and his tendency towards didacticism.

In its broadest outlines, Wilder's humanism is akin to the twentieth-century literary humanism of Irving Babbitt and Paul Elmer More which was such a powerful literary force in the 1920's. While he diverges from the humanism, or "neo-humanism," of Babbitt and More on important issues relating to man's "lower" nature, he agrees with them, as these plays indicate, in their Platonic assumption of dualism—of a "higher" and a "lower" nature in man—and in their concept of the ethical nature and value of the masterpieces of art and literature. Like its predecessor in fifth-century Greece, twentieth-century humanism assumes above all the dignity of man when he acts in accord with the spirit of moderation and rejects absolutes, dogmas, and extremes of passion as dangerous expressions of human disproportion, or *hubris,* that are bound to result in suffering or destruction—in what the Greeks regarded as the retribution of Nemesis.

The humanist position is characteristically tentative because it avoids what More called the "Demon of the Absolute."[3] Even in denying one absolute, More maintained, it is not necessary to lay hold of another. Humanism rejects, therefore, what it regards as the excessive rationalism of the scientific spirit, the extreme reliance upon the feelings of the romantic temperament, and the sentimental humanitarian belief that man can become perfect with social "progress." It insists that man must be guided in life by both reason and the feelings— in proper balance—and that any improvement in the human lot has to be accomplished from within the individual through development of his higher, or ethical, nature, and from restraint of his lower nature, or animalistic passions.

The humanist agrees, however, with scientific naturalists, romantics, and humanitarians that man's powers of reasoning, his feelings, and his social instincts are grounded in nature; but the humanist holds that man also has an ethical sense that transcends the physical and that he both responds and aspires to harmony with a moral and ethical reality above the self. The record of man's ethical aspirations, he maintains, is to be found particularly in the great masterpieces of literature and art of ancient Greece; but it exists also in those of Rome, of the Renaissance, and of the Hebraic-Christian tradition. Ethical perception comes with sensibility and intuition (high imagination) cultivated and sharpened by study of the masterpieces.

But in rejecting the naturalistic contention that man, like the other animals, is merely a part of nature and is governed by the laws of nature, by heredity, environment, and his passions, the humanists of the twenties were confronted with the question of what the final purpose of ethical conduct was to be. T. S. Eliot posed this problem most dramatically and challengingly in 1927 in "Humanism of Irving Babbit": "And what . . . are all these [people who cultivate the ethical will] going to control themselves *for*?"[4] The ethical affirmations of humanism, Eliot maintained, cannot stand without religious justification; for without religion man has no more reason to develop his ethical nature than to give way to his animal impulses.

More also came to recognize that humanism would ultimately have to look to religion for justification; for he rhetorically asked: "Will not the humanist, unless he adds to his creed the faith and hope of religion, find himself at the last, despite his protests, dragged back into the camp of the naturalist?"[5] Eliot wrote: "Humanism is either an alternative to religion, or is ancillary to it . . . it always flourishes most when religion has been strong; and if you find examples of humanism which are anti-religious, or at least in opposition to the religious faith of the place and time, then such humanism is purely destructive, for it has never found anything to replace what it has destroyed." But on the other hand, Eliot added, "Any religion . . . is for ever in danger of petrifaction into mere ritual and habit, though ritual and habit be essential to religion. It is only renewed and refreshed by an awakening of feeling and fresh devotion, or by the critical reason. The latter may be the part of the humanist."

The plays in *The Angel That Troubled the Waters* reveal Wilder's early acceptance of the role of humanistic critic of the moral and theological petrifaction of religious orthodoxy. In "Fanny Otcott" in which the Bishop's prudishness is shown to be a degradation of Fanny Otcott's devotion to life in love and in the last four plays in which believers are warned against both complacency and rationalism, Wilder is the humanistic critic rather than the humanistic philosopher. While he reveals the same general assumptions as the humanists, of dualism, of the moral nature of literature, and of the existence of a higher ethical reality, Wilder shows here the humanistic critical attitude rather than the unified humanistic theories of Babbitt and More. Moreover, his moral affirmations end in faith.

The plays reveal, however, that while he was the critic of religious complacency and moral shallowness, he also accepted responsibility for affirming traditional moral and religious values by confronting rather than evading the most compelling claims of philosophical naturalism against them. These tasks—particularly the second and more formidable one—require much longer and more comprehensive treatment than was possible in such short works; but the first indications of his humanistic intent and of his technical non-realism are found in them. These two essentials are the bases of his subsequent work.

Of the sixteen plays in the volume, only "Fanny Otcott" can be readily staged; for it is set in the present and has a situation that does not involve action so non-realistic that it is physically impossible to present it. Most of the plays are more satisfactory for reading than for performance. They resemble narrative-dramatic poems more than theatre dramas; and, although exquisitely constructed and remarkably compressed and evocative, they are unsatisfactory for the stage.

Wilder spent 1928 to 1930 touring Europe with his sister Isabel and studying the techniques of stage production in Continental theatre—and in one period of sixty-three days he attended fifty-two plays.[6] His interest in the practical aspects of staging indicated his felt need to develop more workable techniques of non-realistic presentation than these plays contain. The stage demands a concreteness and objectiveness and an illusion of living characters that these little plays—drawn from books rather than life—did not have. Wilder was looking for techniques that would permit him to combine his moral and religious themes and poetic style with the demands of the living stage. But he was still primarily a novelist at this point in his career. Because the novel offered the narrative tech-

niques and devices needed to portray the inner life in relation
to the transcendent, eternal truths of the universe, he was
then most successfully achieving in it his aesthetic and moral
aims.

CHAPTER 2

Three Romance Novels

LIKE THE plays in *The Angel That Troubled the Waters*, Wilder's first three novels—*The Cabala* (1926), *The Bridge of San Luis Rey* (1927), and *The Woman of Andros* (1930)—departed from the realism and philosophical naturalism that had dominated the drama since Ibsen and Becque and fiction since Zola and Howells. He was not alone in his departure, for by the twenties non-realistic movements were discernible in both genres. In the novel, Proust and Gide in France and Henry James in America had gone beyond the surface notations of literalist realism and the deterministic limitations of naturalism to a more subjective art based upon intuition. James combined psychological realism not only with fantasy in "The Turn of the Screw" but with symbolism in *The Wings of the Dove, The Sacred Fount,* and *The Golden Bowl;* Proust worked out a careful system of personal symbols in *Remembrance of Things Past*; and Gide was couching humanistic themes in such classical vehicles as the Prometheus myth. All three dealt with moral and ethical themes that realistic, objective records of external phenomena could not convey and which philosophical naturalism could not justify the validity of.

In the theatre, Strindberg had led the revolt against the realism of Ibsen in the latter part of the nineteenth century; and his influence was being felt in the expressionism of the German theatre in the 1920's. In Ireland, William Butler Yeats had tried poetic drama—of which *Cathleen ni Houlihan* was the best known—in the Abbey Theatre of Dublin. And in France Maurice Maeterlinck, Apollinaire, and Paul Claudel had rejected realism for symbolism, surrealism, and poetic religious drama, respectively.

The non-realistic movement that had emerged by the 1920's was rich and varied; and it was to it that Wilder's work was allied. It is noticeable, however, that even in this era the main strength of the non-realistic movement lay outside the United States where naturalism and realism were securely established by Theodore Dreiser, Sinclair Lewis, and Eugene O'Neill and supported by the powerful pen of H. L. Mencken. Such excursions into expressionism as O'Neill's *Emperor Jones* (1920) and Elmer Rice's *The Adding Machine* (1923) and such deviations in romance as James Branch Cabell's *Jurgen* were exceptions rather than the rule. It is not surprising, then, that Wilder's works were regarded as radical departures from the literature of the day although they were part of a wide-spread, vigorous reaction to the realism of the latter part of the nineteenth century.

I *The Cabala*

As Edmund Wilson has indicated, examination of *The Cabala* reveals the influence of Proust[1] in the theme of the hopeless love of the person of superior sensibility (Alix) for one who is unworthy of it (Blair). But the influence of James Branch Cabell and Henry James is even greater than that of Proust. Like Cabell's esoteric romances, particularly *Jurgen,* *The Cabala* brings past and present together in modern and mythological characters but with this difference: Wilder brings his classical gods to the present and suggests their presence in characters drawn with considerable realism; Cabell sends Jurgen back to the ages and places of the myths. The romantic re-creation of mythical characters typical of Cabell's work can be seen in Wilder's drawing of the Cabalists as modern incarnations of Jupiter (Cardinal Vaini), Demeter (Miss Grier), Pan (Marcantonio), Venus and Adonis (Alix and Blair), and Mercury (the narrator). Furthermore, *The Cabala* has an episodic structure unified by themes rather than by action in the manner of Cabell's *Chivalry;* but Wilder's episodes have additional unity because the characters consti-tute a single group.

The influence of Henry James can be recognized in the general outline of the plot, in which an American cultural pilgrim goes to Europe with an admiring—at times naive and romantic—attitude towards it; meets a group of highly cultivated people by whom he is deeply impressed; and learns they are less than perfect but gains a new awareness of the cultural qualities his own country lacks. Like such famous Jamesian people as Mrs. Tristram of *The American,* Maria Gostrey of *The Ambassadors,* and Mrs. Stringham of *The Wings of the Dove,* Wilder's character is the interlocutor and the confidant whose dialogues with the principal characters define them and reveal the roots of their moral conflicts. He is also, in the manner of James's Strether in *The Ambassadors,* the "central intelligence" from whose point of view the narrative operates.

But while these similarities are palpable, Wilder's purposes are clearly not those of Cabell and James. Wilder shares Cabell's desire to use the materials of the classical past in order to get beyond the limitations of literalist realism to the inner world of motives and desires. But where Cabell's characters typically search into the past for an ideal but end with a skeptical attitude to life, Wilder's narrator—likewise looking to the past for an ideal—carries forward into the future the spirit of the old tradition and accepts without disillusion the passing of the old order.

While it is apparent that Wilder was influenced by Cabell's non-realistic techniques, use of fantasy, stylistic grace, episodic structural arrangements, and romantic symbolism, his work is a refutation of a good deal of what Cabell said, especially in *Jurgen.* Wilder's soul-sick Marcantonio is a grim comment on the obsession with sex that pervades Cabell's work and his Alix is a reaffirmation of the higher, aristocratic qualities of an older order of womanhood that Cabell satirized. While Wilder, like Cabell, is concerned with the preservation of Hellenic-Christian culture, he affirms those humanistic principles of restraint and decorum that Cabell attacked, on their obverse side at least, as middle-class taboos.

Moreover, Wilder gives an ironic twist to the well-worn theme of the American abroad. Unlike most of James's people, Wilder's American gains from his European experience a new appreciation of the possibilities of culture in America. While he admires the European cultural tradition, he is not overwhelmed by it; and, when he returns to New York, he takes with him the conviction that a great culture is in the making in America and feels a sense of responsibility for bringing the best in the old culture to bear upon the new one. Such an attitude represents a departure not only from James but from most of Wilder's contemporaries in the "lost generation" as well; for most of them were still some years away from reconciliation with their homeland and some of them never became reconciled with it. The reconciliation in *The Cabala* arises from two dialectically developed conflicts: an historical conflict between past and present; and a moral conflict, growing out of the historical one, between the modernistic spirit of rationalism and materialism and the humanistic spirit of the past.

The main characters of *The Cabala* are a group of Roman aristocrats whose misfortunes symbolize the decline of European culture. The action is reported by a young American scholar—whom the Cabalists call Samuele—who has become their confidant. Parallels between past and present run through the course of the narrative: A dying poet is a twentieth-century version of John Keats; the Cabalists are living in an ultramontane and royalist past; the spirit of Virgil pervades the scene and finally appears to the narrator as he departs for New York.

Living in the past, the Cabalists are in constant opposition with the forces of modernism. The conflict between past and present begins when the narrator, who has come to Rome to study the "ancients," finds them incarnate in the Cabala. While the moral themes develop during the course of five episodes and show the impact of the change in the social order upon the Cabalists, Samuele observes their fall and sees the decay of their admirable culture. In the second, third, and fourth episodes he sees the death of the old aristocratic order (as symbolized by Marcantonio); the impotence of the humane sensibility (Alix) before the indifferent, clinical probings of scholarship without the humanistic spirit (Samuele's fellow American scholar Blair); and the decline of the old vigorous Augustinian or Pauline faith (embodied by the Cardinal) in a Church that has lost touch with life. Finally, in the fifth chapter—when the young scholar-narrator invokes the spirit of Virgil and is told that "The secret is to make a city, not to rest in it"—he realizes that the past, whatever its glories, is dead and that his responsibility is to the present, the future, and to America.

The three episodes that comprise chapters two, three, and four are moral tragedies in which Marcantonio, Alix, and Astree-Luce are victims of both their own anachronism and the modern rationalistic temper. Considering the shortness of the episodes, the chief characters are strikingly individual and their misfortunes deeply moving. The tragedy of the young nobleman Marcantonio, who commits suicide after an act of incest with his sister, is that—endowed with a passionate nature—he has no firm moral and religious code by which to discipline it and give it meaning and purpose. He symbolizes the decay of royalism and aristocracy. His death—like the mythical death of Pan, of whom he is the reincarnation—marks the end of a great period in history; for he is the only male heir the Cabalists have.

The events of the episode establish an impression of the inevitability of his death. Shortly after Samuele meets the Cabala, Marcantonio's mother, the Duchess d'Aquilanera, asks him to help reform the boy, whose sex orgies are becoming a Roman scandal. Having found a suitable aristocratic marriage prospect for him, she wants Samuele to divert him from his debauchery until she can get him respectably married. Considerations of right and wrong in the boy's actions are not involved in her request; she is concerned solely with preventing his reputation from becoming so bad that the marriage will not materialize and the noble line from which he is descended be discontinued. Nor does the Cardinal, who also urges Samuele to help reform the boy for "a month or two," believe any longer in moral behavior. When Samuele accuses him of not really believing in temperance, he replies:

Believe in it. Of course I do. Am I not a priest?
Then why make the boy . . . ?
But after all, *we are in the world*.
I laughed. I shouted with a laughter that would have been insulting, if it hadn't contained a touch of hysteria. Oh, I thank thee, dear Father Vaini, I said to myself. I thank thee for that word. How clear it makes all Italy, all Europe.

Never try to do anything against the bent of human nature.
I came from a colony guided by exactly the opposite principle.

Marcantonio's moral corruption is an inevitable result of the
decline of the ultramontane, aristocratic order into religious
and political impotence. The dominant impression Wilder
presents of the Cabalists is that, while they are all gifted in
one way or another, they have fallen into uselessness; they
retain the wealth, titles, social graces, and religious trappings
of the aristocratic order without accepting its responsibilities.
Robbed of their political and religious responsibilities, the
Cabalists become morally decadent, weak-willed, and de-
fenseless against the social forces that besiege them. Thus
Marcantonio becomes hopelessly caught up in historical and
moral conflicts he cannot contend with.

The network of forces, inner and outer, acting upon him
gives this episode a remarkably complex and intense symbolic structure. The weight of a dead past is upon him in the
obligations his title places upon him; the moral debility of
the declining culture he represents makes him an easy prey
to the moral nihilism of the modernistic international set
whose standards he has adopted; Samuele's Puritan conscience, working upon his latent sense of guilt, ironically helps
drive him to his final act of degradation and then suicide.
The full tragic impact of Marcantonio's death is felt when
his body is found by an officious American tourist, a Detroit
manufacturer named Perkins, who has tried to use his ac-
quaintance with Samuele as a pretext for an invitation to the
Duchess' villa. Though he has been able to buy his way into
Italy's most exclusive cultural sanctuaries, Perkins has not
been able to penetrate the social screen that separates him
from Italy's most exclusive families, the Cabalists. Failing to
get an invitation from Samuele, he steals into the garden of
the Villa, where he finds the body. The vulgarity of the
American Philistine here provides a grim and ironic contrast
to the fallen aristocratic greatness that Marcantonio symbolizes.

The moral decay that leads to Marcantonio's death is tied
directly to the decline of religious faith, which is the theme
of the episode involving Astree-Luce and the Cardinal. In this

episode the clash between the simple, intuitive believer Astree-Luce and the Cardinal, who has lost his faith, results in a crushing loss of faith for her and an agonizing realization for him that he has committed an evil act. Wilder's humanist dialectic here sets the irrationalism of Astree-Luce in opposition to the rationalism of the Cardinal and resolves itself in a synthesis of enlightened faith and love. The Cardinal has lost his faith because, like his colleagues in the Vatican, he has lost touch with life. As a missionary in China he has been a great spiritual power, perhaps the greatest since St. Paul; but the relative isolation and orthodoxy of the Vatican have removed him from the real source of his faith: enactment of his moral principles in living. Deprived of contact with life, his principles have become an intellectual matter to him; and skepticism has won over faith.

Wilder's criticism here is directed not only at the petrifaction of religious orthodoxy—as represented by the "tiresome nonentities" in the Vatican who lack intellectual vigor—but at twentieth-century rationalism which has eaten away the Cardinal's faith and moral belief. The devitalized Church, concerned with matters of form and custom, is largely responsible for the moral and emotional deterioration of the Cardinal to whom faith has become an intellectual game. Detached from the intellectual and social currents of the day, the Church (standing for institutional religion in general) has lost its moral meaning for both Marcantonio and the Cardinal.

Yet the Cardinal himself is responsible for what he does to Astree-Luce to whom he is the greatest living man of faith. When he brings the full force of his great intellect upon her simple, naive faith, he becomes the epitome of evil; for he, misusing the power of his mind upon the feelings of one who lacks his endowment, has failed in his responsibility to those weaker than himself. The Cardinal is aware of the dangers of rationalism and the naturalistic spirit. When the narrator urges him, at the request of Astree-Luce, to write the great book she feels he can write, he refuses and condemns literature that reflects that spirit (Spengler, Frazer, Joyce, Proust, Freud) as "ordure." "What is the matter with this twentieth century of yours. . . ?" he demands. "You want me to compliment you because you have broken the atom and bent light? Well, I do, I do." But, ironically, it is that spirit that prompts him to crush Astree-Luce's faith.

Wilder's position is not anti-intellectual. Astree-Luce herself, the narrator declares, has always illustrated "the futility of goodness without intelligence." She is an intuitive believer, and while at times "she was able to let fall remarkable penetrating judgments," she is unequipped to deal with the Cardinal's rationalism, which, Samuele remarks, "would have had no effect on sound intellectual believers." The humanistic theme of enlightened faith—that is, the theme that religious faith must begin on the human level with love—arises when their relationship is rebuilt on a moral basis. The narrator comments: "When Astree-Luce and the Cardinal discovered that they were living in a world where such things could be forgiven, that no actions were too complicated but that love could understand, or dismiss them, on that day they began their lives all over again." This incident of the Cardinal and Astree-Luce is the most moving one in the book because both characters are deeply involved in the tragedy. The Cardinal, finally realizing the full implications of what he has done, reaches authentic tragic stature when, as an act of contrition, he embarks to resume his work in China but, falling mortally ill aboard ship, asks for burial at sea in order to erase any semblance of identity.

In the "Alix" episode the thematic unity of the book breaks down somewhat; but, next to the Cardinal, Alix is the most complex and compelling character in the book. In this episode the Princess Alix d'Espoli falls in love with Samuele's American scholar friend Blair, is coldly and rudely rejected by him, and suffers heartbreak and humiliation which bring to an end her friendship with Samuele as well as her affair with Blair. This theme, the Proustian one Edmund Wilson has called it,[2] of the agonizing love of a superior person (Alix) for an inferior one, is the central one of the episode; but while there is agonized suffering in the other episodes, this one differs from them because the suffering does not carry with it the concept of cultural decline. That this theme was intended for this chapter is indicated in the beginning when the narrator lists the activities of the Cabala after the death of Marcantonio. These consist of stirring up public opinion about the "faint smell of drains" in the Vatican; sending to Berlin for a tree doctor to save some oaks in the Borghese Gardens; and blocking the advancement in the Church of "several tiresome nonentities." "To tell the truth," Samuele remarks, "their accomplishments were not very considerable. I soon saw that I had arrived on the scene in the middle of the decline of their power." Having tried to deal with matters of greater import in Italy and failed, "they realized that the century had let loose influences they could not stem, and contented themselves with less pretentious assignments."

But the cultural decline is not realized in the main episode itself. Alix, herself, symbolizes the best of the old aristocratic tradition. She "is not really modern"; in her one may "glimpse into the seventeenth century and . . . reconstruct . . . what the aristocratic system must have been like in its flower." However, Blair does not represent anything peculiarly modern, so only half of the past-present conflict is found in the chapter. The tension at the center of the episode is that between sensibility and intellect; and only the former is connected (but *both* are in the following chapter) with the past-present conflict.

Alix, a sort of Jamesian character, is a woman of excellent qualities who is ill equipped to contend with the vagaries of natures not her equal. Most of the third chapter is given to the demonstration of her excellence and to the suggestion of a relationship between a character such as hers and a work of art, a parallel faintly suggestive of James's picture of Milly Theale in *The Wings of the Dove*. Alix is the mime, the artist, who needs the active participation of an audience for the success of her social talents. She has a wound-and-bow talent that flourishes under suffering; and she is most witty and entertaining when her suffering is most intense. Her highly developed sensibility and her wit make her the delight of all—except Blair—who know her.

Blair does not recognize—or does not appreciate—her talents and virtues; and her humiliation at being seen by Blair and Samuele at a séance is the final, crushing blow to her pathetically desperate attempts to find an outlet of some sort for her great spiritual resources. Because of her choice, superstition triumphs over her native intelligence and a balanced sensibility is thrown out of balance. Her profound need for love is never satisfied, and her "exquisite" nature breaks in the presence of Blair's cold intellectualism. This development is the purport of the third chapter.

The moral theme of love is satisfactorily carried by the action, as is the symbolic significance of the dissociation of intellect and sensibility; but the intended tension between time past and time present fails to evolve, and the chapter lacks that important relationship with the others. Despite this defect, the character of Alix is so compellingly drawn that the breakdown in unity tends to be forgotten in reading the chapter. Although there is a good measure of sentimentalism in the drawing of Alix, she stands in the tradition of the Jamesian heroine and does credit to it.

Wilder's attempt to weave together the conflicts between past and present and between traditional moral values and such naturalistic by-products as rationalism, skepticism, and hedonism is only partly successful in *The Cabala*. In addition to the fact that the historical theme is not adequately developed in the Alix episode, there are other violations of unity—most notable of which are a digression about the family history of the American Miss Grier and a portrait of the German Mrs. Berstein, neither of which contributes to the action or themes in any way. Nor are the realism and fantasy brought together in an entirely satisfactory manner. The book begins realistically and the characters and incidents are developed throughout with such compelling realism as individuals that Miss Grier's claim, near the end of the book, that they are the Olympian gods incarnate seems arbitrary and contrived, an unconvincing alteration of the Cabalists from symbols of the past to literal embodiments of it. The intent of Miss Grier's explanation and of the invocation of Virgil is to make explicit the theme that the spirit of the past is alive. But this theme has already been suggested in the symbolic development of the chief characters, and the sudden shift to fantasy and explicit statement reduces the effectiveness of the irony in the simultaneous buildup of the Cabalists as sharply defined individuals and symbols.

Yet from the standpoint of character development this is a

remarkable first novel. Each of the main characters is highly complex and vital, and the episodes dealing with them as individuals have the stamp of authenticity. *The Bridge of San Luis Rey* shows a substantial improvement in Wilder's technical skill, but the characters in *The Cabala* are as powerful and as memorable as any in *The Bridge*.

II *The Bridge of San Luis Rey*

Like *The Cabala, The Bridge of San Luis Rey* (1927) is a romance. Although the fantasy of *The Cabala* is missing, *The Bridge* has the remoteness of setting, the symbolism, the yoking together of past and present, the moral and religious themes, and the episodic structure of the earlier book; and in it Wilder attempts, as he did in *The Cabala,* to capture not only surface realism but the complex workings of the inner life as well. He had stated his conviction that the purely realistic fiction of the day had run the course of its usefulness and effectiveness when he told Harry Salpeter in 1928 that he felt that America was turning away from the rule of realism to the introspective novel. "Until about ten years ago," he told Salpeter, "experience was very valuable as a preparation toward the writing of novels. Authors who had been stokers and barhands did bring something valuable to America in the process of discovering itself. But now the notation of things has been done so well through such men as Sinclair Lewis that from now on the profounder assimilation of a little experience rather than a rapid view of a great deal is the more desirable. Literature, now that America has discovered itself, could spring from solitude and reflection, with less emphasis on observation and more on intuition."[3]

Nevertheless, in both *The Cabala* and *The Bridge* the characters are portrayed with considerable realism and clarity as individuals; and, from the standpoint of response to the promptings of the flesh and susceptibility to forces of environment and heredity, they are conceived with enough naturalism to allay any charges that Wilder ignores the observable and unpleasant facts of life. Marcantonio's losing struggle with his "lower nature," for instance, is as compulsive and has a pathetic consequence similar to that of Clyde Griffith in Dreiser's naturalistic *American Tragedy;* and Camila Perichole in *The Bridge* feels the same physical attraction to bullfighters that Hemingway's Lady Brett Ashley does in *The Sun Also Rises.* The Cabalists and the victims of the disaster at San Luis Rey, moreover, are as subject to the forces of history and circumstance as any characters of Dos Passos or Stephen Crane.

But Wilder's humanism precludes what he regards as the one-sidedness of philosophical naturalism and realism. The characteristic feature of these two novels and of *The Woman of Andros* is the inclusion of the inner as well as the outer facts of life with the intent of reaffirming the sense of the mystery of life which realistic and naturalistic writers had tended to ignore in their concern with external, observable data and with the power of heredity and environment. Wilder gives full scope to the claims of scientific, observable, objective knowledge (as manifested in literature by naturalism); but he insists that the inner life—the passions, the intellect, the hopes and the aspirations—is a mystery whose workings and purposes defy rationalization. The life of the mind is one of constant struggle between the lower and the higher qualities in man. Moreover, that inner struggle has a metaphysical parallel in the universal tension between chance and purpose. This view of course is not original, but the achievement of it in a literary work is difficult. If the work is original, the ideas take on fresh meaning.

Wilder revealed that it had been his intention in these early works to try to restore the aura of mystery to life when he told Walther Tritsch in a Berlin interview in 1931 that "It is the magic unity of purpose and chance, of destiny and accident, that I have tried to describe in my books."[4] The superiority of *The Bridge* over *The Cabala* consists in large part in its more successful achievement of the "magic unity" through dialectic. The action of *The Bridge* begins when Brother Juniper, a Franciscan monk, sees the bridge fall and the five victims plunge to their deaths in the canyon below. "Why did this happen to *those* five?" he asks. "If there were any plan in the universe at all, if there were any pattern in a human life, surely it could be discovered mysteriously latent in those lives so suddenly cut off. Either we live by accident and die by accident, or we live by plan and die by plan."

Convinced the incident is an act of God, he sees in it an opportunity to observe God's intentions "in a pure state"; but, when his investigation of the lives of the victims shows no pattern of cause and effect, he concludes that the "discrepancy between faith and the facts is greater than is generally assumed." Juniper's mistake is that he never learned the "central passion" of the lives of the three adult victims— the Marquesa de Montemayor, Pio, and Esteban. So the omniscient author steps in to recount these intimate facts although he admits that it is "possible that even I have missed the very spring within the spring." We move, then, from the extrinsic motivations revealed by Juniper's investigation to the intrinsic motivations in the minds and hearts of the victims.[5]

Wilder borrowed some of his material for *The Bridge* from Prosper Mérimée's *La Carosse Du Saint Sacrement*. In the Perichole, he combined Mérimée's Perichole with the parrot that taunts her; and he drew the Marquesa de Montemayor after Mérimée's marquise d'Altamire.[6] But it is with Conrad's *Chance*, rather than Mérimée's work, that the book can most profitably be compared. Like *Chance, The Bridge* explores the themes of moral isolation and love and raises the question of whether events occur by accident or design. The title of Conrad's novel is ironic: Life is not a matter of chance or accident.[7] Even where chance appears to govern men's lives— as it does in the events involving Flora de Barral and young Powell—there are causal factors at work. Conrad took as the epigraph for *Chance* a quotation from Sir Thomas Browne: "Those who hold that all things are governed by fortune had not erred, had they not persisted there." While Browne believed that all events have a divine cause, Conrad showed them in *Chance* to be governed by human motivation. He presented a series of incidents that seemed to be the result of sheer chance, but then showed that behind the appearance of accident was an intricate network of human causes. Flora's suicide attempt, for instance, appears to have been caused by a chain of misfortunes that began with her father's financial disaster; but it actually can be explained by her abusive treatment at the hands of the disgruntled Eliza, whose actions can also be explained in terms of clear-cut traits of character.

Wilder's strategy is to set forth the two alternatives by means of external and internal evidence—that which Brother Juniper adduces to prove the presence of the hand of God in the fall of the bridge, and that which he cannot see because it is in the minds and hearts of the characters. Juniper combines the two extreme and dogmatic interpretations of the incident: the scientific, which sees the fall as something that can be explained in physical terms; and the orthodox Christian, which sees in all events the operation of Providence. Both of these views are based upon externals, and Juniper's collection of data in the scientific manner in order to settle a theological question is a *reductio ad absurdum* of both positions, since his investigations lead to no conclusion at all.

Attention is thus directed to the inner sources of evidence when the omniscient author points to the "central passion" in each of the major characters. Beyond this purely human explanation lies the suggestion that there is a divine cause in the "central passion," love, in the victims. The fall of the bridge of San Luis Rey symbolizes the force of circumstance or of the meaningless workings of nature, but the passions of the victims act as the primary human cause leading them to the bridge. Fusion of these two factors brings about the "magic unity" of purpose and chance that provides the element of mystery which is the essence of mysticism. The applicability of the Browne epigraph to *The Bridge* is thus apparent: Those who hold that the fall of the bridge was an accident would not err in their position if they did not insist upon its being the whole truth. To this Wilder adds: Those who believe would not err if they did not insist, like Juniper, upon proving God's presence in all the events of life.

Between the first chapter ("Perhaps an Accident") and the last ("Perhaps an Intention"), three flashback chapters recount the lives of the three chief victims up to the time of the disaster. Each of them, it turns out, is a person with deep spiritual attachments whose "central passion" is thwarted either by emotional coldness or selfishness or by natural circumstance. But each is also governed to such an extent by his consuming passion that the conflict it generates and the disaster that follows it have the earmarks of fate. Yet each one is a free spirit and has an opportunity, just before the fall of the bridge, to make a compromise with the circumstances of his situation and rebuild his moral life. The vision is a tragic one: Their deaths are an inescapable fact, regardless of the interpretation one makes of their lives; but their deaths are not entirely futile, since they generate a love in the survivors that did not exist before.

The sense of mystery is achieved in the episodes dealing with the individual victims, whose complexity demonstrates why Juniper's investigation is futile. The Marquesa de Montemayor has fixed her whole spiritual being upon her daughter, Dona Clara, who has married a Spanish nobleman to escape her mother's extreme affection. Cold and intellectual like her father (and like Blair in *The Cabala*), Dona Clara is the opposite of the Marquesa, whose love for her daughter is the chief factor in her life. Dona Clara sails from Peru to Spain "with the most admirable composure, leaving her mother to gaze after the bright ship, her hand pressing now her heart and now her mouth."

The object of her life gone, the Marquesa turns in upon herself and lives a mental drama in which she and her daughter live as she, the Marquesa, would have them live. "On that stage were performed endless dialogues with her daughter, impossible reconciliations, scenes eternally recommenced of remorse and forgiveness," the Marquesa always being the one who forgave and the daughter feeling remorse. To the people of Lima there was no indication that the Marquesa was suffering the agonies of the unloved. They knew her as a slovenly, drunken old woman who talked to herself; at one time there was a petition circulated to have her locked up, and she had been denounced by the Inquisition. They were unaware, when interviewed by Juniper, that she read widely and that she wrote letters to her daughter (letters Wilder patterned after those of Madame de Sévigne) which "in an astonishing world have become the textbook of schoolboys and the anthill of grammarians." These letters, like all great literature, reflected "the notation of the heart."

But while genius was concealed by outward ugliness and kindled by suffering, the Marquesa had moral weaknesses that were a part of the love that generated the great letters. For one thing, her devotion to her daughter was "not without a shade of tyranny: she loved her daughter not for her daughter's sake, but for her own." And even the great letters, in their sophisticated tone of detached amusement at the people and events in Lima, concealed the lack of humility and courage in the love that produced them. The Marquesa learns the lessons of humility and courage from the orphan girl Pepita, who also dies in the disaster.

Pepita, whose devotion to the Abbess, Madre Maria, is as strong as the Marquesa's for Dona Clara, is sent by the Abbess to serve the Marquesa. Feeling as strongly about her separation from the Abbess as the Marquesa does about hers from her daughter, Pepita writes a letter to the Abbess asking to return to the convent. She does not send the letter, however, because she feels it "wasn't brave." The Marquesa, having read the letter, discovers in it the humility and willingness to sacrifice that she herself lacks. The night before the fall of the bridge, watching Pepita as she sleeps, the Marquesa whispers to herself, "Let me live now . . . Let me begin again."

The Marquesa's "central passion" gains an added dimension by her apparent victory over circumstance. Like Pepita, she has had an unfortunate beginning in life, Pepita being an orphan, the Marquesa having had an unhappy childhood. Pepita, however, since coming under the guardianship of the Abbess, has lived in an atmosphere of love and sacrifice that has enabled her to withstand the affliction of separation with courage, which the Marquesa was not able to do without losing her religion and seeking escape in drinking. The Marquesa's life has been directed by circumstance up to the time she reads Pepita's letter, since, in addition to having a daughter who is colds towards her, her selfishness and lack of courage both stem from an unhappy childhood and a marriage she was forced into against her will. When she decides to "begin again," therefore, she affirms the triumph of her will over circumstance. Yet, ironically, she seems to lose to circumstance finally when the bridge falls.

The complex development of the Marquesa's character

and the interplay between the forces of will and circumstance preclude any easy metaphysical or theological affirmations. The episode ends in mystery, as do those involving Esteban and Pio. But the moral imperative of love is clear enough; and the highest love is the kind of disinterested love shown by Pepita and by the Abbess, whose life is devoted to the care of the suffering. The levels of love are worked out in a somewhat broader fashion in the Esteban chapter and represent Wilder's humanistic answer to the contention that love is a purely human contrivance.

At the lowest level are Camila's shabby, clandestine affairs with various men of Lima. She hires Manuel to write letters to her lovers, all of whom she quarrels with and almost casually abandons. In contrast to her animal-like passion, vulgarity, and absence of profound feeling is Manuel's brief but intense love for her. Manuel himself is not inexperienced sexually; for both he and Esteban "had possessed women, and often, especially during their years at the waterfront; but simply, Latinly." His love for Camila, however, represents a departure from purely physical pleasure: ". . . it was the first time that his will and imagination had been thus overwhelmed." That is, he rose for the first time to a human level in love and above the mere promptings of nature. He "had lost that privilege of simple nature, the dissociation of love and pleasure." Understanding nothing higher than physical pleasure, Camila is cynical about love. "There is no such thing as that kind of love," she tells Pio. "It's in the theater you find such things." But Manuel, without art or learning, has no such cynicism. Love is as natural to him as pleasure, but more intense, and in it one undergoes a "crazy loss of one's self." He represents an affirmation that love may spring from a higher source than sexual desire.

He shows an even higher type of love than this love for Camila in giving her up for the sake of Esteban. Again, there is no intellectual analysis, no reflection, in his sacrifice. He intuitively feels the isolation of Esteban; and, while his attachment to him is not so complete as Esteban's for him, it is strong enough to make Manuel willing to sacrifice to save his brother from misery.

Yet profound as Manuel's devotion to Esteban is, it falls

below Esteban's for him. If Manuel's love is characterized by sacrifice, Esteban's is characterized, after Manuel's death by blood poisoning, by the complete identity of himself with his brother. But Esteban discovers in Manuel's attraction to Camila "that secret from which one never quite recovers, that even in the most perfect love one person loves less profoundly than the other. There may be two equally good, equally beautiful, but there may never be two that love one another equally well." Esteban's love attains the level of the tragic, for it is a part of the human condition that "the most perfect love" is never quite perfect.

This ascending scale of types of love, culminating in Esteban's devotion to his brother, sets the stage for Captain Alvarado, who has also suffered a loss, that of a daughter. The cause of the girl's death is not mentioned, but it is implied that there is no more "reason" for it than for Manuel's. The captain's grief is as profound as Esteban's, but they react in opposite ways. The captain travels "about the hemispheres," as the Marquesa writes to Dona Clara, "to pass the time between now and his old age." Yet he is reconciled to life, is determined to live it out to its end, and even hopes to see the girl again. Esteban cannot, however, face life or reconcile himself to it without Manuel. His identification with Manuel is so complete that he buries himself, figuratively, and assumes Manuel's name; and the night before the bridge falls, he attempts suicide. The inability of Esteban to face life without his brother symbolizes the pathos of man before circumstance. Endowed with a profound capacity for love and for pain, Esteban is unable either to comprehend or to accept a world which cares for neither. When the captain asks him to sail aboard his ship, he accepts in the hope that he can escape from his hopelessness in ceaseless activity. But this hope is short-lived: He cannot leave Peru, where Manuel is buried.

By the end of the Esteban episode, the moral qualities that comprise the highest form of human love appear in the acts of courage, humility, and sacrifice performed by the victims prior to the fall of the bridge. In the Pio episode, love is seen in terms of its highest and most concrete expression in art. The theme of artistic beauty being wrested from ugliness through the agency of love, a minor theme in the Marquesa episode, is developed fully in the Pio chapter. When Pio decides to "play Pygmalion" with Camila, his three great passions—"his passion for overseeing the lives of others, his worship of beautiful women, and his admiration for the treasures of Spanish literature"—assume moral significance. Until he meets Camila, Pio is totally unscrupulous. The conflict that develops when he begins to train her for the stage is the conflict between the artist (it is he, more than Camila, who is the artist) and his recalcitrant materials, the raw life from which the artist creates. Camila is Pio's "great secret and reason for his life"; but she is "quite incapable of establishing any harmony between the claims of her art, of her appetites, of her dreams, and of her crowded daily routine." Each of these is "a world in itself, and the warfare between them would soon have reduced to idiocy (or triviality) a less tenacious physique." Lack of a profound love to integrate the various claims upon her leaves Camila without any real meaning in her life. She lives almost at random, the theatre at times capturing her enthusiasm, love at others; but nothing lasts for long, including her love for the Viceroy, whose mistress she becomes. Once during the twenty years she and Pio are associated love comes into her life—when she first meets the Viceroy—and then her acting reaches its perfection.

Pio's attempts to bring art and life together in a perfect union in Camila are successful only when love is present to bridge the gap between the two. This would be a platitude if it were not for the fact that the love that informs both is accompanied by suffering. This profoundest love, Pio believes, is a "cruel malady through which the elect are required to pass in their late youth and from which they emerge, pale and wrung, but ready for the business of living." He has the humility and compassion that come from the "illness" of love—the "rich wisdom" of the heart that Camila does not find until she has lost her beauty (by smallpox), Pio, and her son Jaime.

Having thus defined love and the abstract qualities that give it moral significance, Wilder concludes the book with the theme of love as a moral responsibility. All the survivors realize their failure to respond to the love directed toward them, imperfect though it was in the cases of Pio and the

Marquesa. The full impact of love as a first condition to meaningful living comes to all the survivors after the disaster; and
the Abbess, the only character in the book whose life has
fulfilled itself in love (although even she, as she confesses
to herself, has been too busy to appreciate fully the devotion of
Pepita) expresses the significance of love in a world meaningless and purposeless without it: "Even now . . . almost no
one remembers Esteban and Pepita, but myself. Camila
alone remembers her Uncle Pio and her son; this woman
[Dona Clara], her mother. But soon we shall die and all
memory of those five will have left the earth, and we ourselves shall be loved for a while and forgotten. But the love
will have been enough; all those impulses of love return to
the love that made them. Even memory is not necessary for
love. There is a land of the living and a land of the dead and
the bridge is love, the only survival, the only meaning."

Limited as it is to the human level, this proposition is
directed to believers and skeptics alike; it warns both that,
whatever their beliefs about God, love is indispensable if life
is to have any meaning. The question raised by Juniper remains a mystery; the "perhapses" in the titles of the first and
last chapters remain. At one level, human motivation brought
the victims to the bridge at the same time—and in this *The
Bridge* resembles *Chance*—but these motives have been shown
to be so bound up with circumstance that the two are hardly
separable. Moreover, as Juniper's investigation shows, the
"good" died with the "bad"; there was no discernible relationship between desert and reward. Moral behavior, Wilder
maintains, is, therefore, a purely human responsibility and
has clear-cut human consequences: Whatever the interpretation of the disaster, it generated in the survivors a love that
had not previously existed.

The theological and metaphysical question remains, however, in the "magic unity" achieved in the mysterious synthesis
of circumstance and human motivation; and the sense of
mystery in the lives and deaths of the characters provides
an option for both believer and non-believer; at the same
time the mysterious is in itself, paradoxically, the basis for a
mystical interpretation. With regard to the persuasive effect
of "magic unity"—which it was Wilder's declared aim to

achieve—Kenneth Burke has remarked: "Mystery is a major resource of persuasion. Endow a person, an institution, a thing with the glow or resonance of the Mystical, and you have set up a motivational appeal to which people spontaneously ('instinctively,' 'intuitively') respond. In this respect, an ounce of 'Mystery' is worth a ton of argument."[8] This mystery in the lives of the characters convinces rather than the "arguments" set against one another by Juniper. Thus, while Wilder doesn't say it in *The Bridge,* the "spring within the spring"—the love that bridges the land of the living and the land of the dead—has mystical significance.

The Bridge has often been charged with being sentimental, but there are really no grounds for such a charge because Wilder gives full enough scope to the weaknesses of the characters to preclude the expenditure of any undue feeling for them. Furthermore, there are no tears of happiness at the end of their suffering; their love in each case brings pain, and, finally, death. Nor is the book so optimistic as it might seem to be at first reading.

Yet *The Bridge* is not an unqualified success as a novel. Its most noticeable weakness is the episodic structure which, though thematically unified, obviates progression in a single narrative line. Characters are developed in one episode only to be dropped almost entirely in the next one and replaced by a new cast. Another weakness—its most important technical one—is the sometimes obtrusive presence of the omniscient author, who judges and interprets as he narrates the histories and inner lives of the main characters. This subjective, arbitrary narration weakens the dramatic structure of the book, although it is compensated for to a considerable degree by the fact that the dramatic scenes embody or suggest much of what the omniscient author says about the characters. Wilder was aware of the defects of omniscient author narration and came to favor the stage over the novel as an art form partly because he was convinced that dramatic narration eliminates the subjective presentation that he felt was inherent to the novel.

Still, there is a strong dramatic quality to *The Bridge;* and the proclivity for direct, objective presentation that was to lead Wilder to turn his attention in the thirties primarily to playwrighting can be seen in such passages as the following where the character of Pio, the loving but obsessed perfectionist taskmaster, comes through—as does the imperious, cruel but childlike nature of Camila—in dialogue and short-view narrative:

> At the close of a performance Camila would return to her dressing room to find Uncle Pio whistling nonchalantly in one corner. She would divine his attitude at once and cry angrily:
> "Now what is it? Mother of God, Mother of God, what is it now?"
> "Nothing, little pearl. My little Camila of Camilas, nothing."
> "There was something you didn't like. Ugly fault-finding thing that you are. Come on now, what is it? Look, I'm ready."
> "No, little fish. Adorable morning star, I suppose you did as well as you could."
> The suggestion that she was a limited artist and that certain felicities would be forever closed to her never failed to make Camila frantic. She would burst into tears:
> "I wish I had never known you. You poison my whole life. You just think I did badly. It pleases you to pretend that I was bad. All right then, be quiet."
> Uncle Pio went on whistling.
> "The fact is I know I was weak tonight, and don't need you to tell me so. So there. Now go away. I don't want you around. It's hard enough to play that part without coming back and finding you this way."
> Suddenly Uncle Pio would lean forward and ask with angry intensity, "Why did you take that speech to the prisoner so fast?"
> More tears from the Perichole: "Oh, God, let me die in peace! One day you tell me to go faster and another to go slower. Anyway I shall be crazy in a year or two and then it won't matter."
> More whistling.

Each of Pio's passions is manifest in these lines: "his passion for overseeing the lives of others, his worship of beautiful women, and his admiration for the treasures of Spanish literature," which Camila was enacting. And Camila's sloth, her vulgar arrogance, but withal her driving obsession for perfection and her despair at not achieving it, and the hint that her exasperation will lead her finally to less arduous pursuits—all are found in this dialogue.

The Bridge has become a classic of American fiction, and it will likely continue to hold a high place among that very august company of novels written during the twenties by such men as Lewis, Hemingway, Fitzgerald, and Dos Passos—different as it is from their works. Despite its technical weaknesses, it has all the intellectual scope, depth of feeling, and complexity of character that make a mature and aesthetically satisfying vision. It was an unusual, courageous act in the twenties for a serious writer to affirm the moral nature and value of love—a subject most serious writers were associating in one way or another with sex. The almost inherently banal and sentimental "higher" manifestations of love were being abandoned to the hack writers or rejected as "genteel." But as he defines love in *The Bridge,* it is a most difficult thing; for it is accompanied by selfishness, confronted by human coldness, and lost upon a universe that does not seem to know or care that it exists. Considering the critical climate that prevailed in the twenties, it might fairly be said of Wilder himself what he says in *The Bridge*: "There are times when it requires high courage to speak the banal." *The Bridge* shows that not only courage but also the touch of the poet is there. The familiar takes on new life and meaning in art.

III   *The Woman of Andros*

The Cabala took place in Rome, 1920; *The Bridge* in Peru, 1714; and Wilder's third novel, *The Woman of Andros,* went farther back in time and place to pre-Christian Greece. Published in 1930, *The Woman* appeared at an unpropitious time, for the depression was under way and the climate of opinion was not favorable to fiction that ignored current economic and political problems. Understandably, the book failed with both the critics and the public.

But the depression was not the only factor contributing to its failure; it had its own serious defects. Wilder was becoming increasingly derivative as he went back in time. In *The Bridge* he gave the material he borrowed from Mérimée the flavor of his own developing narrative genius, but in *The Woman* he reverted to the aestheticism and "poetic" style that characterized the three-minute plays and to the subjective mode of presentation that had marred the generally objective presentation of *The Cabala* and *The Bridge*. Furthermore, the irony that brought complexity to the earlier novels was absent from *The Woman*, as was the element of dramatic realism which gave the themes of these books concrete embodiment and integration in action. Operating on two thematic levels, the moral and the historical, *The Woman* did not successfully weave those themes together. The historical theme, represented by the coming of Christ, was thrust into the story arbitrarily at the beginning and the end.

Of course the book is not the failure this list of weaknesses makes it appear to be. If it lacks the dramatic intensity of the other works, it has the virtues as well as the infirmities of that poetic, non-realistic side of Wilder which has distinguished him from most of his contemporaries. But as is true with most important writers, his artistic virtues and vices are closely allied—and Wilder's vices generally are his virtues in excess; in *The Woman* the author's skill in fine writing draws undue attention to itself. The concise and evocative qualities of his style, for instance, are present; but they descend at times into sententiousness and, on occasion, into preciousness.

The Woman is Wilder's most direct attempt in a novel to show the religious propensities of the classical Greek humanistic temper. The first part of the book is based upon Terence's comedy, *The Andria*, which in turn was based upon two lost plays of Menander. A short book, *The Woman* is a simple story involving many of the same characters of the Terence original: a Greek boy Pamphilus, his father Simo, the hetaira Chrysis (the "woman"), and her younger sister Glycerium. Wilder left out, however, such of Terence's characters as Davus, Charinus, and Dromo; and he altered the story to suit his own religious-humanistic purposes. His Glycerium, for example, is really the sister of Chrysis; Terence's only pretends to be and is actually the daughter of the merchant Chremes. Also, Wilder does not solve Pamphilus' problem, as Terence did, by having it discovered that the pregnant Glycerium is the daughter of Chremes. Nor is there a *homo ex machina* such as Crito to save the day. Wilder's Pamphilus has to face the facts that Glycerium is the sister of a hetaira and that she is pregnant. And, finally, Wilder's Glycerium dies, as Terence's does not. As these changes indicate, Wilder made a serious novel out of Terence's comedy.

But while he discarded the love affair of Charinus and Philumena, Wilder retained the Terentian "double plot" by placing beside the love affair of Pamphilus and Glycerium the conflict between the humanistic Chrysis and the "respectable," conventional citizens of Brynos. Chrysis symbolizes the spirit of classical Greek culture; she is Socratic (and, in fact, quotes Socrates at length) in her approach to life, in her spirit of inquiry, and in her having a group of young disciples. Like Socrates, she is at odds with society; but, being an outcast and unconfused and uncomplicated by social conventions, she is able to live and observe life in its pure state. With her, Pamphilus—her most intelligent but least vocal disciple—is looking for the meaning of life.

Along with a Captain Philocles (who, like Captain Alvarado in *The Bridge*, has lost a daughter and is "filling the hours in anticipation of release from a life that had lost its savor"), they find that only when they have "died to themselves" and thus rid themselves of "that self that supports the generality of men, the self that is a bundle of self-assertations, of greeds, of vanities, and of easily offended pride," can they begin really to live. Chrysis' home is a refuge for the oppressed and the weak—all who suffer. Like the Abbess in *The Bridge*, she finds that life means nothing except what self-sacrifice and love impose upon it. But she is pre-Christian, and there is no higher justification or sanction for her higher impulses. "Someday," she says, "we shall understand why we suffer. I shall be among the shades underground and some wonderful hand, some Alcestis, will touch me and will show me the meaning of all these things. . . ." The source of suffering is shown here, as in *The Bridge*, to lie in the conflict between external circumstance and self-preoccupation on the one hand and the internal world of "love, virtue, and wisdom," which only a very few people cultivate, on the other. The tragedy of life consists in the realization that one is failing in the latter. Chrysis finds that it is "true, true beyond a doubt, tragically true, that the world of love and virtue and wisdom [is] the true world and her failure in it all the more overwhelming."

Chrysis represents the classical humanistic spirit attempting to translate its ideals into action and searching for a final justification in religion for its values. When she dies, she is concerned lest she die like an animal rather than a human being. Her humanity has come from the culture of fifth-century Greece which above all affirmed human dignity; and her greatest concern is to retain that dignity even in the face of death. Although her values lack divine sanction until the birth of Christ, Chrysis yearns for higher justification for her moral principles: "If only the gods were sometimes among us. To have nothing to go by except this idea, this vague idea, that there lies the principle of living." But she dies before the coming of Christ, which, we are told in the first and final paragraphs of the book, is shortly to occur.

Malcolm Cowley has rightly called *The Woman* a Greek pastoral. Its heightened diction, quiet tone, and spare, classical structure give it the qualities of a narrative poem. Almost in the manner of a pastoral elegy, it evokes a mood of quiet melancholy. The island of Brynos, where the action takes place, is a land of natural beauty and the happiest, but "one of the least famous islands" of Greece. The scene is quiet as the story opens: "The earth sighed as it turned on its course; the shadow of night crept gradually along the Mediterranean, and Asia was left in darkness."

But there is an uneasiness, a tension, in the air behind the quiet. "A confused starlight, already apprehensive of the still unrisen moon, fell upon the tiers of small houses. . . ." This tone of quiet apprehension, maintained throughout the book, points to the arrival of the "precious burden"—the birth of Christ—that is soon to come. The tone shows itself in the characters, too, who live in quiet desperation. Chrysis, who is happy temporarily because of her love for Pamphilus (a love destroyed, incidentally, by circumstance—a chance meeting of her sister and Pamphilus which results in their falling in love), says: "I am happy because I love Pamphilus—Pamphilus the anxious, Pamphilus the stupid. Why cannot someone tell him that it is not necessary to suffer so about living."

But she herself suffers as Pamphilus does: "And a low exasperated sigh escaped her, the protest we make at the preposterous, the incorrigible beloved."

Character portrayal develops out of this stylistic and structural tension. The conflict is inner; the characters are unable to achieve a harmonious balance between their own inner compulsions towards beauty, virtue, wisdom, and love and the world they live in. Style and structure join to convey their turmoil and calm, their despair and hopes, the calm of their meditation, and the emotional intensity of their highly developed sensibilities. It is these qualities in Pamphilus and Chrysis that give them what Simo calls "the secret of living." Observing the priest of Aesculapius and Apollo, who is like them, Simo says: "People like that have some secret about living. Why don't they tell it to us outright, instead of wrapping it up in a mystery and ceremonial? They know something that prevents their blundering about, as we do. Yes, what am I doing here . . . but playing the fool? Blundering, advising in things I know nothing about . . . Pamphilus has some of that secret too. And that woman from Andros had it, too . . . there is something of the priest trying to make its way in him." These people stand in contrast, as Simo's words show, to characters like Chremes and Sostrata, Pamphilus' mother, who are bound to themselves and to the kind of social convention that, for example, would compel Pamphilus to marry a girl he doesn't love. Simo recognizes their superiority in sensibility, in love, in compassion, and in their wisdom that comes from their higher sensibility; and his final acceptance of Glycerium into his home marks the beginning of his humanity.

The moral is clear enough. Exquisitely as *The Woman* is constructed—and it wouldn't do to underestimate its poetic qualities—the characters resemble philosophical concepts too much to be convincing as living, actual people. Most of the tension arises from internal monologues, and there is a good deal of philosophizing without corresponding embodiment in concrete, realistic action. *The Woman*, like the three-minute plays, stands as evidence of both the excellence and the inadequacy of the romantic and poetic side of Wilder's vision.

Lacking a counterpart in realistic, objective presentation of external conflict, this side of his vision falls into sentimentalism and his characters take on the coloration of romantic *Welt-schmerz*. The poetic tendencies of the style—effective as they are—and the intrinsically romantic nature of the materials tend to render the moral and religious themes remote from actual life and reduce their claim to serious consideration. In order to be convincing, themes such as Wilder's require the inclusion of some degree of direct, actual experience. Unleavened and untested by a presentation of their antithetical elements, they lapse into sentimentality and romantic mysticism and lack the inclusiveness a fully developed vision should have.

Looking back over this period of his early works, Wilder told Ross Parmenter: "For years I shrank from describing the modern world. I was alarmed at finding a way of casting into generalization the world of doorbells and telephones. And now [1938], though many of the subjects will often be of the past, I like to feel that I accept the twentieth century, not only as a fascinating age to live in, but as assimilable stuff to think with."[9] He actually began to "accept" his own time soon after *The Woman* was published; for in November, 1931, a year after it appeared, he brought out his first works dealing with contemporary America: *The Long Christmas Dinner and Other Plays in One Act*. His extreme swing away from aestheticism (that is, poetic treatment of intrinsically poetic materials derived from literary sources rather than life itself) to comic irony, contemporary American settings, and greater realism in these plays indicates his awareness that these latter elements were needed as correctives to the romantic sentimentalism, remoteness, and stylistic preciousness that had plagued his third novel.

Whether or not the Gold attack had anything to do with this change is hard to determine. It is possible that it—and the attacks a year earlier by the literary radicals upon his intellectual kinsmen, Irving Babbitt, Paul Elmer More, and Norman Foerster—convinced Wilder that it was time to bring his humanism out of the museum he had consigned it to in *The Woman* and into dynamic relationship with his own time. In any case, these plays reveal that he was probing at this time for a mythical structure and a technical method that would enable him not only to provide a faithful representation of the facts of American life but to reveal the spirit of religious humanism which he felt was still alive in America.

CHAPTER 3

Towards an American Perspective

IN HIS interview with Walther Tritsch in 1931, Wilder declared that "the real Americanism that will be important in
the future is belief in the significance and even in the concealed implications of every event. It is precisely the same
thing as the much abused doctrines of predestination and in-
ward asceticism. In daily life this belief sometimes takes well-
known, grotesque forms, such as when the money one has
earned is looked upon as proof of God's mercy or justice.
But that is only the ridiculous side of a very deep and fruitful life feeling. Just think of what it means to every American
to believe himself permanently, directly, and responsibly
bound to world destiny. The significance that this belief im-
parts to the simplest dealings and simplest events seems to me
the beginning of all achievement. Such a trend precedes all
great cultures."[1] Wilder's extensive study of the theatre in
Europe during this period, along with his growing conviction
that America and modern life could provide him with suitable
literary material, brought him the technical and philosophical
foundations he needed to bring his themes to the present and
his drama out of books and onto the stage.

I *The Long Christmas Dinner*

The plays in *The Long Christmas Dinner* (1931) represent
his first successful work for the theatre. The narrative elements
that made most of the three-minute plays difficult if not impossible to stage are either not present in this volume or are
incorporated into the action by use of a chorus-narrator. Set
in the present and involving for the most part American char-

acters of unpretentious origin, these plays comprise Wilder's closest approach to realism in the theatre, his first attempt at a colloquial style, his closest approach to conventional plotting, and his first successful attempt at the dramatic fusion of non-realistic and realistic materials.

"Love and How to Cure it," "Queens of France," and "Such Things Only Happen in Books" all have well-made plots or slice-of-life presentation; and "The Long Christmas Dinner," "Pullman Car Hiawatha," and "The Happy Journey to Trenton and Camden" reveal theatricalist elements later perfected in *Our Town* and *The Skin of Our Teeth*. The first three of these plays are realistic in the sense that the presentation is objective, prosaic, and slice-of-life as opposed to the subjective, religious, poetic presentations of *The Angel That Troubled the Waters*. The themes are still moral, subjective, and aesthetic in the manner of the three-minute plays; but they arise from actions presented objectively enough to be enacted.

Moreover, the characters of these one-act plays develop with enough individuality to be identifiable as specific persons rather than one-dimensional embodiments of abstractions; and they gain complexity through irony. The central character of "Queens of France," for example, is a swindling New Orleans lawyer named Cahusac who defrauds simple, romantic-minded and spiritually impoverished women by telling them they are the lost successors to the French crown. The action takes place in a specific place (New Orleans) at a specific time (1869). Like the lawyer, the three women who come and go during the action are individualized as well as typed. As gullible, spiritually starved types they are absurd: Each becomes more hilariously arrogant and imperious as she grows more convinced that she is indeed the Queen of France; and of course the more convinced each one becomes, the easier it is for Cahusac, as "representative of the Historical Society in Paris," to get her contributions towards the Restoration. As an individual, each makes her own peculiar response to her "rise" in station. But while the women are ridiculous, they are also pathetic because of the emptiness which makes them susceptible to Cahusac's fantastic story. Comic irony turns to pathos near the end of the play when Cahusac discards the schoolteacher, Mlle. Pointevin, who has run out of money.

She says: "It is all very strange. You know, M'su Cahusac, I think there may have been a mistake somewhere. It was so beautiful while it lasted. It made even schoolteaching a pleasure . . ."

More didactic but likewise ironic is "Love and How to Cure It," a realistic fable about love. As in "Queens of France," its theme arises from a concrete action involving specific, individualized characters. A medical student named Arthur has threatened to kill a shallow Cockney girl, Linda, who has spurned his love. The plot consists of the efforts by Linda, her Aunt Rowena, and Joey—all theatre people—to dissuade him. Arthur enters with a revolver hidden beneath his opera cape; and, during the action, Joey, a comedian, convinces Arthur that people who shoot the persons they love really love themselves and want to be noticed rather than loved in return. Arthur learns his lesson and leaves. But while he is repulsive to Linda because he is so "hot and excited and breathing so hard," it is Linda—"impersonal, remote, almost sullen"—who, in her cruel repudiation of the passionate Arthur, is the more culpable party and represents the same reprehensible coldness to love that characterized Dona Clara in *The Bridge* and Blair in *The Cabala*.

While these two plays show Wilder bringing some of the irony of his first two novels to the stage, "Such Things Only Happen in Books" reveals his increasing awareness that his works would henceforth have to deal more directly with life as he observed it. This play is a satire about a writer who, oblivious to the teeming life about him, complains that he has no plots for his stories. He has too much "literary conscience" to use such banal plots as "The plot that murderers always steal back to the scene of their crime and gloat over the place," or the plot that "all married women of thirty-five have lovers." Such things, he maintains, only happen in books. "Books and plays," he says, "are a quiet, harmless fraud about life." Believing that life really has no such interesting plots, he is totally unaware of what goes on about him: His wife is having an affair with the young doctor who is treating their maid; the maid has been burned accidentally by her escaped-convict brother, whom she has been hiding in the novelist's house; and a man who murdered his father several years before returns to get the money hidden in the novelist's house, but his sister has already been there and taken the money with the unwitting help of the novelist.

The "well-made," complicated plot of this play is used only once again—in *The Matchmaker,* where Wilder parodies this type of plotting. While he retained the lesson the play taught about the artist's looking to life for his materials, he wanted a greater realism than such artificial plotting could give. He wanted to portray both the specific action and the universal idea imbedded in it, and contrived plotting of external events did not serve this purpose. The other three plays in the volume reflect his attempt to bring together the concreteness of incident and character that mark the above-mentioned plays with non-realistic technical devices. "The Long Christmas Dinner," "Pullman Car Hiawatha," and "The Happy Journey to Trenton and Camden" are works in which he tries for the first time to affirm the presence of universal religious and moral values in the everyday lives of Americans.

His theories of drama were worked out in the making of these plays, and they are ones that accommodate a vision in which the microcosm of ordinary American life is related to what he called "the All, the Everywhere, and the Always." His interest in the expressionism of Strindberg and Elmer Rice during his visit to Germany with his sister Isabel in 1930 shows that he was aware of the Scylla and Charybdis of too much and too little realism in the drama and wanted to avoid both. After seeing a production of one of Strindberg's works, for instance, he maintained that its failure was due to an excess of realism. On another occasion he observed that Rice's *Life Is Real* was too much of a thesis play; the ideas overwhelmed the action and reduced it to mere illustration. What he wanted was both the technical freedom that expressionism could offer and the faithful presentation of life and conventional restraints of concrete realism—"reality," as he wrote later,[2] rather than verisimilitude.

The dramaturgy Wilder developed in these three plays is what John Gassner has called "theatricalism."[3] Its outstanding feature is its frank admission that the action on stage is a play and not the representation of actual life that realism purports to achieve. Wilder stated, in the introduction he wrote for *Three Plays*, that he became dissatisfied with the theatre in the 1920's because he was "unable to lend credence" to what he regarded as the "childish attempts" of the realistic theatre "to be real." The drama, he said, is "based upon a pretense and its very nature calls out a multiplication of pretenses." What he objected to specifically in realistic stagecraft was the presence of properties and settings which he felt detracted from the frankly make-believe nature of stage drama. All that was needed for a good play was a "platform and a passion or two." "Have you ever noticed," he asked, "that in the plays of Shakespeare no one—except occasionally a ruler—ever sits down? There were not even chairs on the English or Spanish stages in the time of Elizabeth I."[4] More positively, he believed that the theatre should be like a festival—in the tradition of the classical Greek theatre—with the audience playing a role either as participants or as vitally involved observers for whom life is being interpreted.

"The Long Christmas Dinner," "Pullman Car Hiawatha," and "The Happy Journey" adumbrate the theatricalism that came into full flower in *Our Town* and *The Skin of Our Teeth*. The circular form of "Dinner" and the stage manager device and the bare or nearly bare stage of the other two plays are deliberate affronts to "fourth wall" realistic attempts to approximate actuality. In these three plays his purpose is to "make the opaque matters of everyday transparent, with a view . . . to discovering something."[5] Each of the plays is based upon everyday matters—often the most trivial ones—in which "something" is discovered. Events in the lives of the characters are presented objectively, for the most part, but are related to a larger cosmological and metaphysical framework by unrealistic stage techniques. In "Pullman Car Hiawatha" and "The Happy Journey" a Stage Manager—a latterday chorus—sets the stage or interprets the action, while in "The Long Christmas Dinner" a cyclical or circular form suggests a relationship between the recurring events on stage and "destiny."

The theme that the smallest events of ordinary life have a significance beyond what they seem to have thus arises out of the conflict between the realistic and non-realistic modes of presentation. In order to get beyond the surface "appearance" of meaningless trivia, Wilder demolishes its claim to reality on the factual, concrete level, and puts the action on a moral, philosophical, or theological level. Hence, in "The Happy Journey" the characters, a humble American family, take a trip in an automobile that consists of four chairs set upon a low platform on a stage which has no scenery. The characters are engaged from the beginning in ordinary, "unimportant" activities. At the opening the boy Arthur is playing marbles, the girl Caroline talking to some friends, Ma Kirby putting on her hat. The dialogue is not heightened in any way. It is the everyday speech of unsophisticated, simple people:

> MA: Where's your pa? Why isn't he here? I declare we'll never get started.
> ARTHUR: Ma, where's my hat? I guess I don't go if I can't find my hat.

The journey to Camden includes such common events as stopping at a gas station, eating hot dogs, and reading billboards, and has as its purpose a visit with the daughter Beulah. But the verisimilitude of slice-of-life is absent because it is destroyed as the play is enacted—by presence of the Stage Manager, by pantomime of the actors, and by absence of scenery and real properties.

Thematic and dramatic purposes come together by this method as the "Act in Eternity." The audience is constantly reminded that what they are seeing is theatre, not actual life, that life is being interpreted, not shown as actuality. The journey to Camden is a happy one, paradoxically, because these unimportant events are important, being by implication significant events in a meaningful cosmological process. Ma Kirby, the central character, attaches a moral-religious meaning to each incident, which either raises her children to heights of joy or throws them into depths of depression. The comic-ironic tone with which she is portrayed restrains the potential seriousness of her moralizing and religious sentimentalism. Her moralizing and sentimentalism are, in fact, lightly satirized—because they are conscious. The real meaning of her life is seen when she is not self-consciously moral in what she does—in her ecstasy, for instance, at Arthur's remorse for having offended her; and in her singing, at the end, the song

> There were ninety and nine that safely lay
> In the shelter of the fold,
> But one was out on the hills away
> Far off from the gates of gold.

She is consciously moral—like Mrs. Antrobus, later, in *The Skin of Our Teeth*—and consciously religious in her attitude and reactions to actual, concrete incidents and things; but she is unconsciously moral in relation to her *real* purposes. The truth of her life lies in what she is not entirely aware of (she sings the song "absent-mindedly")—but which the audience sees. Ma Kirby's simple faith sustains her, gives her courage, and keeps her family going. She tells her daughter, whose baby has died at birth: "God thought best, dear. God thought best. We don't understand why. We just go on, honey, doin' our business." The theatricalism here, breaking through external appearances, supports the idea that Ma Kirby's real virtues lie beyond her superficially moralistic exterior.

"Pullman Car Hiawatha," the most ambitious and intricately constructed of all these plays, has a symphonic structure which conveys the theme of universal harmony. The Stage Manager is used here as the arranger and interpreter of the action, manipulating the characters and scenes according to the idea he wants to illustrate. As in "The Happy Journey" he plays various parts besides his own, without any attempt at realism or individuality. After marking off the outlines of the train on the stage floor, he calls the actors in, director-like, and they enter carrying chairs to their "berths" or "compartments"—their respective marked-off places. The illusion of verisimilitude is, therefore, destroyed before the play begins, just as it is in "The Happy Journey."

But while in this play the family is individualized to some extent, the characters in "Pullman Car Hiawatha" are frankly types: "a maiden lady," "a middle-aged doctor," "an engineer going to California," an insane woman, a young couple, Harriet and Phillip. For, since the play is an allegory, the characters are types who fit into a scheme of ideas. Beginning with the dialogue of these de-individualized types (they are called by their positions on the train—"Compartment Two," "Lower Three"), the play proceeds from the chaotic life in the berths to the sound of the characters thinking—above which their individual thoughts are heard as soliloquies. The characters in the berths are busy with the trivia of life, as seen from the outside, but with more important, personal matters within their minds. In the opening movement the Stage Manager, directing the action like an orchestra conductor, calls for the scene to shift to the compartments and their occupants Philip, Harriet, and the Insane Woman. The last two characters are suffering physically and mentally, respectively. At Harriet's death, the Stage Manager steps in again to direct the car's position "geographically, meteorologically, astronomically, theologically considered."

At this point, a second movement begins in which there is an ascending scale of sounds and rhythms, from the insects in the fields the train passes through to the music of the spheres, all of which join in a universal harmony. Personified are a town (Grover's Corners, Ohio), a field with all its animal and insect life, and the ghost of a workman killed while working on a bridge. Together with a tramp who sings a line from "The Road to Mandalay" by "Frank W. Service," these personifications represent the rhythms and sounds of life measured in minutes—of life as flux without apparent order. The Stage Manager says: "The minutes are gossips; the hours are philosophers; the years are theologians. The hours are philosophers with the exception of Twelve O'clock, who is also a theologian."

The hours, "beautiful girls dressed like Elihu Vedder's Pleiades," carry Roman numerals onto the stage and speak lines from Plato (Ten O'clock), Epictetus (Eleven O'clock) and St. Augustine (Twelve O'clock). Then the planets arrive, each with its individual sound made by the actor playing the part, and the sounds of the earth (all the characters in the play) join with those of the planets.

The third movement begins when the Insane Woman breaks in on the earth's "sound" with the words, "Use me. Give me something to do." She is led back to her guardian, whereupon the Stage Manager announces the entrance of the archangels and the "theological position of Pullman Car Hiawatha." The music motif continues and the sounds of the characters and planets resume to serve as the background for the dead Harriet's recitation of a prayer—and all make up the sound of the solar system. In each of the three movements the rhythms of life blend into harmonious relation with a larger whole—first the earth, then the universe, and finally the solar system. The most humble of the human characters, the tramp, directs the latter part of the second and third movements "like the conductor of an orchestra," the function the Stage Manager fulfills in the first movement and most of the second.

Counterpointing the harmony in each movement are the two sufferers, Harriet and the Insane Woman. Harriet, like Emily Webb in *Our Town*, comes to realize the blindness of humans to the gift of life; and, having been unaware of it and ungrateful for it herself, she protests to the Archangels Michael and Gabriel that she is unfit to go with them—she wants to be punished. The Insane Woman, whose insanity reveals itself in her dialogue with the attendant and the nurse in the first movement, displays insights sane persons lack in her dialogue with the two archangels. In their thematic dissonance, these two characters serve the double functions of emphasizing the ignorance of human beings of their "position" as part of a harmonious, meaningful whole (life, like Pullman Car Hiawatha, has a destination) and of illustrating the Old Testament (Job) and Greek (particularly Aeschylus) concepts of purpose in suffering. That they are in compartments rather than berths, as the other characters are, signifies, perhaps, their special nature as persons having the wisdom of those schooled by affliction.

This remarkably constructed allegory, combining all levels of time and space and relating the life of the mind to the life of the universe, is of all the early plays the closest to *Our Town* and *The Skin of Our Teeth* technically and thematically. In the later, full-length plays, however, Wilder utilizes the concreteness of the individual family found in "The Long Christmas Dinner" and "The Happy Journey" to achieve a more realistic microcosm than he achieved in this play. Absence of an adequate dramatic focus deprives "Pullman Car Hiawatha," one feels, of sufficient tension. Its movement is musical, blending discordant or dissonant elements into harmonies which dissolve conflict instead of intensifying it. Wilder's vision in this play of an harmonious universe in which all contradictions are ultimately resolved has the weakness that critics like Brooks and Tate find in "Platonic" poetry: Its propaganda is exclusive, too easy, and oversimplified rather than inclusive. One admires the theatrical novelty but is not persuaded by its propositions.

Wilder did not follow up these first dramatic ventures into the contemporary American scene until 1938 when *Our Town* appeared. In the meantime he translated and adapted a play that was thoroughly anti-realistic—Obey's *Lucrece*, for Katharine Cornell in 1932—and wrote his most realistic novel, *Heaven's My Destination* (1935). The mythical structure that would permit him to combine a convincingly objective view of American life with a non-realistic portrayal of its relation with human destiny was still to be formulated. But if by 1935 he had not yet found the vehicle to carry his conviction that the great universal humanistic values could be found in American life, he was able to diagnose the moral illness of mid-depression America in humanistic terms in one of the best but least appreciated novels written in that era of proletarian and humanitarian panaceas, *Heaven's My Destination*.

II *Heaven's My Destination*

What *The Woman of Andros* had lacked more than anything else was an effective and concrete antagonist to its main characters to give dramatic tension and expression to their inner conflicts. The spiritually torpid society that failed to understand and appreciate Chrysis and Pamphilus was inadequately developed, with the result that the humane concepts they embodied were not clearly defined in action and that their longings for religious certitude and for a greater human consciousness in love appeared maudlin. Wilder corrected this weakness in *Heaven's My Destination* (1935) by shifting to the American scene and drawing it fully and realistically.

The chief character, George Brush, is a kind of Elmer Gantry in reverse; and it is possible that Wilder intended the book to be in part an answer to Lewis. Like Gantry, Brush gets his early religious training in a Baptist college in the Middle West, has an early sexual experience with a girl from a small town, and runs into difficulty with believers and non-believers alike. But unlike Gantry he is a sincere believer himself; and, where Gantry profits from his unctuousness, Brush suffers for his true belief. The sarcasm Brush en-counters as a believer is reminiscent at times of the tone Lewis used towards Gantry and his fellow clergymen. But while Gantry lives in an America of false belief and hypocritical clergymen, Brush lives in a nation that has lost its spiritual heritage and sense of purpose. Moreover, Wilder's book has a compassion mixed with satire that gives it a far more subtle irony than is found in *Elmer Gantry*.

By providing a clear-cut conflict between an individualized character and a society that reacts vitally to him, Wilder achieves his themes through concrete action rather than by dogmatic assertion. The point of view is so objective, in fact, that the book was criticized unfavorably for failing to state unequivocally the author's attitude toward Brush. Wilder told Ross Parmenter in 1938: "My last novel was written as objectively as it could be done and the result has been that people tell me that it has meant to them things as diverse as a Pilgrim's Progress of the religious life and an extreme sneer-ing at sacred things, a portrait of a saint on the one hand and a ridiculous fool jeered at by the author on the other."[6] The fact is that the objective presentation itself is ironic: Brush is both a fool and a saint, and the humanistic themes are not stated but must be inferred from the dialectical development of the action. Despite the general failure of the reading pub-lic and the critics to understand the book, Wilder maintained his conviction, as he told Parmenter, that "the ultimate point of view . . . the beholder should take upon the action [in a literary work] is nowhere indicated, but is distributed through-out the work by a series of strains and stresses in selection and emphasis."

The "ultimate point of view" in *Heaven's My Destination* arises from the conflict between the fervent humanitarianism and religious fundamentalism of George Brush and the ma-terialistic society he tries to reform. Out of the conflict emerge the features of the humanistic ideal of human perfection. Briefly, the historical framework of that ideal and the assumptions behind it are as follows: Like Babbitt and More, Wilder holds that men must return to the classical Greek and Renaissance conception of men as distinct from both nature and God. During those great periods of human history, human perfection (the Greeks called it *areté*) was the accepted cultural aim. Presupposed in the goal of human perfection were belief in the dignity of man, in his position of primacy in the universe, and in the free will and responsibility of the individual. Man was thus neither a tool of the gods nor a helpless prey of nature—though admittedly he was profoundly affected by both. Perfection in fifth-century Greece consisted of full development of all the human powers, physical, emotional, and intellectual—each restrained from excess by the others and by the fear of *hubris*. Perfection during the Renaissance subsisted, again, in the achievement of excellence in learning, in cultivation of the intellect and the moral sense through study of the Greek and Latin masterpieces, in control of the appetites and passions, and in conduct of the affairs of life in accordance with the rules of reason.

Humanists, from Matthew Arnold in the nineteenth century to Babbitt and More in the twentieth century, have held that the ills of modern man are caused by departure from the goal of human perfection. Western civilization turned in the wrong direction, Babbitt claimed, when naturalism, which came about with the rise of science after Bacon, drifted to the opposite extreme from pre-Renaissance theological monism—to a monism that regarded man as purely a part of nature. The result was that men turned their attention from themselves as men (that is, from the classical Greek and Renaissance ideal of perfection) to the study of nature and its uses. Two general intellectual movements thus developed: sentimental and scientific naturalism. The first of these was manifested in the romantic movement of the eighteenth and nineteenth centuries, with its sentimental view of nature and man as a part of nature. In the romantic view—which Babbit maintained was epitomized by the philosophy of Rousseau—man was held to be inherently good but corrupted by his environment. Human nature, therefore, was held to be ameliorable through improvement of environment. Humanitarianism came about when this belief in the innate goodness of man turned to pity for the plight of the common man and when demand for social reform displaced belief in individual responsibility.

Scientific naturalism, the second intellectual movement to rise in the post-Renaissance period, shifted the attention of men from self-perfection to concern with matter and force; and with its experimental method, science eliminated traditional moral and ethical values from its field of knowledge. The results were a sterile rationalism, a technological society in which men were reduced to narrow specialists, and a metaphysical view of man that regarded him as an unimportant cog in the cosmological machine.

The humanistic reaction against the imbalances of modern society began with the powerful writing of Matthew Arnold, who argued for "culture"—for a revitalized humanism and against the "anarchy" of a dehumanized and demoralized civilization. Among other things, Arnold set his pen against the reformism of the English liberals, who would have given the task of achieving human perfection to the state; and against the rationalism of science—as defended by Thomas Henry Huxley—which would have replaced the ethical authority of classical literature with application of the scientific method to moral matters. Arnold contended that what was needed was a restoration of the balance between intelligence, which reformers lacked, and moral concern, which science and technology had all but destroyed. Post-Darwinian in his thought, Arnold also regarded traditional theology as lacking in "light," or intelligence. Culture, human perfection, he believed would have to take the place of religion. His lonesome battle in the nineteenth century was carried on in its general aspects by Babbitt and More in America. And in the 1930's, five years after a critical attack by a Marxist (who represents a combination of both sentimental and scientific naturalism), Wilder continued the fight with the full force of his irony in *Heaven's My Destination.*

Wilder's Brush, a Midwestern Baptist, moral reformer, and book salesman, represents an amalgamation in their most innocuous and comical forms of the fundamentalist, the humanitarian, and that archetype of the materialistic society, the salesman. He symbolizes what one critic called "America in its awkward age,"[7]—an America attempting naively to reconcile its disparate spiritual and materialistic qualities. Brush's innocence is the naivete not only of the fundamentalist who rejects the theory of evolution and insists upon a literal interpretation of the Bible but also of the humanitarian who, ignorant of evil, is betrayed by both his own lower impulses and those of others to commit acts he regards as sinful. The action—set in the Midwestern Bible Belt, stronghold of evangelism—takes place during the depression of the 1930's when humanitarian panaceas for reform were perhaps more prevalent than at any other period in American history and when the nation was suffering most from the materialistic binge of the 1920's. The clash that results when the ingenuous but spiritually healthy Brush brings his religious and moral principles to bear upon a society sick with skepticism and moral apathy is at once comical and pitiful.

Out of that conflict arise the implied themes of a faith purified of ignorance, of moral principles based upon both tolerance of human frailties and understanding of evil, and of skepticism tempered by moral concern. Brush symbolizes both the best and the worst in the American religious and moral tradition. He can sell books even during a depression; but he finds that the religion he tries to peddle has almost no market. During the year covered by the novel, he makes a sales tour of the Middle West and Southwest and meets a cross-section of society which rejects his preaching and moralizing. His futility is a compound of absurdity and well-meaning goodness. His religion has come to him by way of conversion during his sophomore year in college by a sixteen-year-old girl who, he learns later, was a drug addict. His courses at college have included "How to approach strangers on the subject of salvation" and "Arguments in Sacred Debate." Thus armed with both evangelical fervor and the know-how of salesmanship, he accosts people he meets with "Brother, can I talk to you about the most important thing in life?" At one point his belief in *ahimsa* (influence of Gandhi) leads him to try to help a hold-up man avoid arrest, which Brush regards as a form of cruelty. His attempt fails; and, when Brush is brought to trial, the judge, who is one of the few characters in the book who are aware of the virtue as well as the naivete of Brush's theories of *ahimsa* and voluntary poverty, tells Brush without irony: "Well, it's all sort of poetical and sentimental, Mr. Brush; but it's very unlike the facts of life. And it seems to be based upon a profound misunderstanding of the criminal's mind."

Far as Brush's religious and humanitarian principles are from the "facts of life," they are humane; and if he exasperates people almost beyond endurance, he also helps some of them, even after they have mistreated him. He promises to take responsibility for the child of a dying man who has almost cruelly abused him, for instance, and saves another from self-destruction at the risk of his own life.

Society, Wilder makes it clear, needs Brush and his values, whatever their weaknesses. The people Brush meets are typically sophisticated and cynical on the surface but resigned to despair beneath it; and they can find no way out of their perdition. Among the people he encounters are a man named Roberts at Camp Morgan, who has nightmares and is nearly mad with worry; three roomers at a Kansas City boarding house who despise Brush because he is a constant reminder of their own spiritual emptiness; a disillusioned intellectual, Burkin, who scorns Brush's religious naivete. Invariably they become angry with Brush and abuse him but fail to change him to their ways, which they try to do as much as Brush tries to change them. He also comes into conflict with such social institutions or problems as banks, prostitution, and the depression; and by his transcendence of the particular type of bondage they represent—that is, to money, of the flesh—he infuriates those who are their victims, willing or unwilling.

But the fact that Brush's otherwise admirable humanitarian and fundamentalist principles lack intelligence is suggested by his conflicts with intelligent people in the incidents involving Jessie Mayhew and Burkin. In the first of these incidents Brush becomes fond of the bright young college girl until he learns that she "believes in" evolution: "Brush almost whispered: 'You don't think the Bible'd tell a lie, do you? Do you mean you can't see there's a difference as big as the whole world between a human being with a soul and a monkey jumping around in a tree?' There was an awful silence. Then Brush put another fateful question: 'You don't believe in women smoking cigarettes, do you?'" The girl refuses to discuss these absurdities with Brush and dismisses him from her mind—though not without difficulty.

But the intellectual Burkin does discuss them with him. An unemployed motion-picture director who has been mistakenly jailed as a peeping-tom, Burkin, brilliant and cynical, is the opposite of Brush. He is contemptuous of the Bible, the bourgeois, and Brush. After Brush has related his religious and evangelical experiences, Burkin says: "You live in a foggy, unreal, narcotic dream . . . Listen, benny, can't you see that what you call religion is just the shiverings of the cowardly? It's just what people tell themselves because they haven't got the guts to look the facts of life and death in the face. If you'd gone to a respectable college you'd have had the chance to get wise to these things. You've probably never been exposed once in your whole life to anybody who really had any practice in thinking."

This rationalistic lecture has too much truth about Brush to be dismissed as name-calling. Burkin's skepticism is a necessary corrective to the extremes of Brush's faith. One is reminded here of Emerson's thesis about Montaigne that the cause of belief is served by a healthy skepticism and, again, of Arnold's concept about the balance between "sweetness" and "light." Burkin's intelligence, inadequate as it is by itself, is the indispensable counterpart to Brush's faith. In his attack, Burkin strikes at the most vulnerable points in Brush's religion: "Burkin plunged into primitive man and the jungle; he came down through the nature myths; he hung the earth in astronomical time. He then exposed the pretensions of subjective religious experience; the absurdity of conflicting prayers, man's egotistic terror before extinction."

Yet, like most of the others Brush meets in his travels, Burkin is a sick spirit; his sickness—cynicism—is manifested by a "nervous twitch" he cannot hide. And in the conflict between his rationalism and Brush's fundamentalism the higher synthesis is enlightened faith. Brush's immediate reaction to Burkin's attack is: "When you began I thought you were going to say things that would stick in your mind and trouble me"; but then he adds: "you don't know anything about religion until you start to live it. All you've done is *think* about it as though it were . . . as though it were a *fish* a long ways off." So they separate unreconciled, thought and feeling, reason and intuition, intelligence and morals, each needing the other; they are unresolved antitheses whose fusion is unlikely to occur until Brush's fundamentalist faith and humanitarian morals establish themselves on a sound humanistic foundation. In his present state of awkwardness Brush is unequipped to deal effectively with his opposition. His inability to distinguish the real sources of evil, for example, leads him to spend his time and energy combatting such minor sins as smoking by women; at the same time he is being gulled by acquaintances who have taken him to a house of prostitution. During his brief loss of faith following the breakup of his short-lived marriage, he observes bitterly that: "I've broken all the Ten Commandments, except two. I never killed anybody and I never made any graven images. . . ."

Wilder thus directs his double-edged satire towards the kind of Elmer Gantry cynicism seen in Burkin and Brush's fellow boarders in Kansas City on the one hand and Brush's naivete on the other; he attacks by implication both the doctrines of social amelioration and human perfectibility so dear to humanitarian reformers (including Marxists like Gold) and the spiritual sterility of rationalism. Noticeably absent from this proletarian-age novel is any suggestion of class conflict or of the presence of economic or natural forces that overwhelmed the "common man" in such outstanding novels of the day as Steinbeck's *In Dubious Battle* and *Grapes of Wrath*, in which the two major skeins of sentimental and scientific naturalism come together. Steinbeck's books define the human plight in terms of the misuse of nature, both physical and human. Nature rebels against the over-cultivation of the Oklahoma topsoil in *The Grapes of Wrath;* and this depletion and the predatory economic system drive the hapless farmers from the land they love. Steinbeck's implied solution to the problem is social: Political and economic reforms are needed to restore the balance between man and nature, between a bountiful nature and the men who are instinctively a part of it but who are forced, because of economic circumstances, to misuse it.

Wilder's diagnosis of the human condition is, however, moral, inner. While Brush does come into conflict with a bank manager by refusing to collect interest on his savings, he also maintains: "No one who has saved up in a bank can really be happy." This implies that fear—a moral matter—is the ultimate reason that such economic "forces" as banks exist. The power of such temporal forces would not exist if the fear they feed on were abolished. Although such a view does not solve the problems of the dust-bowl farmer or the factory worker who is at the mercy of economic cycles, it attacks indirectly the immorality of a social system that preys upon human frailties and it prescribes moral strength as the real solution. Eliminate the moral causes—fear, greed, cynicism toward human motives—and the power of any economic system, of nature itself, over human life will be greatly reduced.

Such a program, Wilder indicates, is a matter of individual will. Human perfection and the sense of purpose that accompanies the *desire* for human perfection are Wilder's humanistic ideal and prescription for the ills of America. That ideal is suggested by what Brush will probably become. His humanitarian moral fervor, nourished by an evangelical faith, represents "goodness" in its "awkward age"; for Wilder chose as his epigraph a passage from *The Woman*: "Of all the forms of genius, goodness has the longest awkward age." Brush's generosity, his devotion to the spiritual and material welfare of others, and his desire to conduct his life by a moral code rather than by acceptance of the world as he finds it comprise some of the basic elements of that ideal.

His main weakness is, therefore, that of both humanitarianism and fundamentalist faith: lack of intellectual maturity. His development towards maturity is slow; but, since he does develop, there is hope that he will fulfill his promise. His conflicts indicate that he will retain his faith but that it will be strengthened by a supporting intelligence. He learns in the course of his travels, for example, that belief in evolution may not be immoral. At the end of the book he goes through a "crisis" that leads him into temporary disbelief; but after his faith is renewed by an expression of confidence in him by another man of faith—a dying Catholic priest whom Brush never meets—he continues with the same activities he pursued at the beginning, except that now he meets a waitress who is reading Darwin and arranges to put her through college. Purged of some of their worst elements of ignorance and narrowness, his faith and morals are more secure as the story ends; and he is considerably more prepared for the "business of living" than before. The great gulf between the humanistic ideal as Wilder conceives it and the "real" facts of American life is not bridged here, and Wilder gives no indication that it will be; but he leaves no doubt that it can be. If it is to be done, faith based upon humanistic ethics is requisite.

Heaven's My Destination is in the tradition of *Candide, Tom Jones,* and *Huck Finn* in its episodic picture of an innocent taking a journey that brings him into contact with various facets of society. It is Wilder's most realistic novel; and his masterly handling of point of view enables him to achieve a vision which affirms much the same values as those of *The Woman,* but without its sentimentalism, and which satirizes both his hero and his society without lapsing into the sarcasm and caricaturism that marred *Elmer Gantry.* While one should not miss the deliciously humorous ways Brush exasperates people, it would be a mistake to take the book as a joke, as some critics did, at a time they felt to be unsuited to jokes. It is as serious as *Candide* and *Huck Finn*—nearly as serious in fact as *Pilgrim's Progress.* And while Wilder undoubtedly had great fun elaborating the traveling-salesman–farmer's-daughter story into a full-length work, his picture of the various illnesses of contemporary society is as grim as it is comical. And because it does not limit itself to such specific problems of the thirties as Pittsburgh and the breadlines, it escapes both the topicality and the oversimplification that have sent many of its contemporaries in fiction into oblivion. Furthermore, it does what many satiric novels fail to do: It lets us sympathize with all the characters as fellow human beings, for Wilder loves his people even when he satirizes them most severely.

CHAPTER 4

Three Theatricalist Plays

IN THE FALL of 1930 Wilder accepted an invitation from his ex-classmate at Yale, Robert Hutchins, to teach at the University of Chicago. Wilder taught at Chicago for six years. In 1935 he himself invited Gertrude Stein to give a series of lectures; and, as might be expected, he became her most admiring friend and disciple. They had long conversations which Wilder later summarized in part in introductions to her *Four in America, Geographical History of America,* and *Narration: Four Lectures.* She taught him, he recounted later, to ignore the critics and to write "as though no one else were listening"[1]—useful advice for a sensitive person like Wilder who had already suffered from virulent critical attacks and was to undergo more in the next decade. More important, she enabled him to bring his aesthetic theories and humanism into cohesion and to apply them affirmatively to contemporary American society.

I *Gertrude Stein and Wilder's Literary Theories*

Everything, including the statement of Professor Wager at Oberlin that every great work was written this morning, "fell into place as he listened to her" wrote a *Time* reporter after an interview with Wilder.[2] She confirmed his humanistic conviction that the eternal human truths were to be found in literary masterpieces, and she then put forth the corollary that those truths can also be observed in American life. She made a distinction—which corresponded roughly to the dualistic one of humanism between body and mind—between human nature and human mind. Human nature, she said, clings to "self," to identity, to location in time and place, and to survival; but human mind, in Wilder's words, "knowing no time and identity, can realize [a non-self situation] as an objective fact of experience."[3] Human mind contemplates pure existing and pure creating, she maintained, and can be observed in masterpieces which record the timeless and universal; but it can also be seen in the America which has always identified itself with world destiny.

While Wilder portrayed the mystical identification of the American with human destiny in its naive form in *Heaven's My Destination*, it was in *Our Town* and in *The Skin of Our Teeth* that he set it forth in conjunction with his fully developed theory which, because of its nature, found the stage a more suitable medium than the novel. This theory and the part Gertrude Stein played in helping Wilder formulate it can be seen in his introductions to her three books on America and in his "Thoughts on Playwrighting," which he wrote in 1941 for Augusto Centeno's *The Intent of the Artist*.[4]

Recalling his conversations with Gertrude Stein, Wilder said in his introduction to *Four in America* that her distinction between human nature and human mind first arose when they discussed the qualities peculiar and common to great writers. Great writers, he said, glossing Stein, possessed a "certain relation to the problems of identity and time." The masterpiece gets its materials from human nature but is of the human mind; and contemplation of the literary masterpiece effects "pure existing" in the sense that the human mind emerges and perceives the eternal and universal in the individual. This human mind that emerges from masterpieces and reveals the truth latent in the minds of all men also appears under certain geographical conditions, she maintained. Wilder wrote: "Miss Stein, believing in the intermittent emergence of the Human Mind and its record in literary masterpieces to be the most important manifestation of human culture, observed that these emergences were dependent upon the geographical situations in which the author lived. The valley-born and the hill-bounded tended to exhibit a localization in their thinking and an insistence on identity with all the resultant traits that dwell in Human Nature; flat lands or countries surrounded by long straight lines of the sea were conducive to developing the power of abstraction."[5]

Gertrude Stein maintained that the American, in his detachment from time and place, is the best living source of evidence of the eternal existing in the individual. In the United States the human mind is "distributed throughout the people," where the writer may observe it in the daily life of ordinary people. Thus while the realistic writer, by implication, tends to confine himself to the literal recording of human nature, the less insular and more imaginative writer —the producer of masterpieces—uses human nature as his materials but goes beyond its surface appearance to the realm of human mind or of eternal ideas.

His acceptance of Gertrude Stein's essentially Platonic view of twentieth-century America—and the relative failure of *Heaven's My Destination* to gain critical and popular favor—convinced Wilder that drama is superior to fiction as an art form because the theatre audience sees "pure existing," while the reader of fiction is asked to accept what the author says arbitrarily *about* the life he presents. In "Thoughts on Playwrighting," he listed "four fundamental conditions of the drama" that distinguish it from the other arts. In combination with the theories of America derived from Gertrude Stein, they show the aesthetic bases of *Our Town* and *The Skin of Our Teeth*. The conditions are: that the theatre performance requires many collaborators; that it is "addressed to the group mind"; that it is "based upon a pretense and its very nature calls out a multiplication of pretenses"; and, finally, that the action "takes place in a perpetual present."

Of the first of these conditions he stated that, unlike the novel or painting, the drama is not the "product of one governing will"—of the artist or the author. Collaborators such as actors and directors, who are vital to drama, necessarily mean variation in interpretation of a play, which of course is a problem to the playwright. The disadvantage is compensated for, however, because "the theater presents certain vitalities of its own so inviting that the writer is willing to receive them in compensation for this inevitable variation from an exact image" and because "the dramatist through working in the theater learns not merely to take account of the presence of the collaborators, but to derive advantage from them; and he learns, above all, to organize the play in such a way that its strength lies not in appearances beyond his control, but in the succession of events and in the unfolding of an idea, in narration."

The audience witnesses the play as a succession of events illustrating a general idea, and through the "disposition of events" the author maintains a control over the idea "so complete that the distortions effected by the physical appearance of actors, by the fancies of scene painters and the misunderstandings of directors, fall into relative insignificance." Because of the "expectancy of the group mind," the problem of time, the absence of a narrator, and the "element of pretense," the drama "carries the art of narration to a higher power than the novel or epic poem." Confronted with the possibility of misinterpretation, the writer is forced to attend to the "laws of narration, its logic and its deep necessity of presenting a unifying idea stronger than its mere collection of happenings."

Wilder felt he could achieve in the drama what he had been trying to do in the novel without complete satisfaction to himself: eliminate the author from the narrative scene and allow the characters to reveal themselves by means of (1) "highly characteristic utterances, (2) concrete occasions in which character defines itself under action, and (3) a conscious preparation of the text whereby the actor may build upon the suggestions in the role according to his own abilities." The author provides some signs of individuality for the actor to go by, but he leaves much of the individual interpretation to the actor and concentrates his efforts upon the achievement of the general idea. The presentation is, therefore, more objective than in the novel because the "dogmatic assertions" of the omniscient novelist about his characters are eliminated. The result is that the stage can do a better job of combining the particular and the universal truth.

In elaborating the second condition of drama, Wilder maintained that because the theatre is addressed to the group-mind, it is a kind of ritual or festival in which the audience is an indispensable part of the production. Without an audience a play would "fall to pieces and absurdity," for the excitement of pretending requires a throng. The audience is both spectator and participant; thus in *The Matchmaker* the characters—like the Stage Manager in *Our Town*, Lily Sabina in *The Skin of Our Teeth*, and the Watchman in *The Alcestiad* —address the audience directly. In theatricalist style the audience is reminded that it is seeing a play. But, he admitted, "a group mind presupposes if not a lowering of standards, a broadening of the fields of interest." Drama cannot assume, as the other arts can, a trained audience capable of understanding or being interested in special aspects of life, such as the historical or the psychological, that are not generally known. If the audience is to play its part in the "festival" that is the theatre, it has to have before it material it understands.

This last point has been a source of irritation to critics— notably to Francis Fergusson[6]—who feel that Wilder compromises his art by trying to please or make himself understandable to the mass mind. What Fergusson forgets, however, in applying T. S. Eliot's standards to Wilder, is that Wilder does not have the contempt for the group mind that Eliot does; and his philosophy does not, in effect, exclude the minds his art tries to teach. The question of whether or not Wilder's appeal to the group mind represents a lowering of standards in drama depends ultimately upon whether or not the material that makes such an appeal is successfully integrated in a vision that does not oversimplify or falsify the life it represents. Fergusson contends that there are two sets of materials in *Our Town* and in *The Skin of Our Teeth*; one set is directed towards the "greater number"; and the other, the philosophical, towards those of greater understanding. Fergusson also asserts that both plays suffer from this division; but the presence of two sets of materials is debatable—particularly in the case of *Our Town*. It is true, however, that both plays use subjects that consciously draw upon common experiences in the audience at all levels. The artistic effectiveness of this device is discussed in relation to these plays later in the chapter.

Wilder's third "condition"—that the theatre is a "world of pretense"—was his refutation in principle of "slice-of-life" realism. He contended that, since the theatre is a world of pretense straining towards a general truth, scenery and sets which tie the action to a specific time and place and which are intended to effect a fourth-wall realism tend to deprive the audience of its imaginative participation and require it to accept as real what it knows is not. The great drama of Greece and China and of Racine and Corneille is cited as evidence that scenery and sets are not necessary to "reality," which Wilder distinguishes from the verisimilitude of realism. In this, of course, he was supported by Aristotle, who placed scenery last in the hierarchy of parts of a play, and by the Chinese, whose classic drama had only placards to identify the scenery.

In explaining the fourth condition for drama, Wilder reiterated his belief that it is a higher type of narration than the novel. "A play visibly represents pure existing," he said. "A novel is what one mind, claiming to omniscience, asserts to have existed." The "pure existing" depicted by the drama made it for him the natural vehicle to express his mythical view of the "pure existing" American, which he had clarified during his association with Gertrude Stein. He felt that such a dramaturgy conjoined with such a mythical vision could restore the festive or ritual atmosphere that the theatre had always had in its greatest ages. At its best the stage play was a kind of religious ceremony in which the audience contemplated the ritual demonstration of the human condition and of the relationship of the individual to nature, to humanity, and to the cosmos.

In an introduction he wrote for the Heritage edition of *Oedipus Rex*, he expressed regret that the great religious experience felt by Greek audiences is missing from the theatre of today. The theatre, he said, "has lost one of its most powerful effects—the shudder and awe induced by the presence of the numinous, by the *tremendum* of religious experience . . ." While Apollo was not in *Oedipus,* Wilder maintained that his presence was felt and that his will was the real subject of the play. The present age is not one in which a religious shudder and awe is likely to be felt as the Greek audiences felt it, but *Our Town* and *The Skin of Our Teeth* are attempts to recover for modern audiences the feeling that there is a meaningful relationship between the individual and nature and mankind and the universe, and to restore to life those elements of mystery and love that are the basis for the affirmation of a higher presence.

II *Our Town*

Such a monumental ambition would be pretentious if handled in a grand manner and on the grand scale. But *Our Town* is pitched in a low key, has an almost pastoral setting, and involves the ordinary events in the lives of ordinary people; and *The Skin of Our Teeth* has strong elements of comedy and burlesque to counterbalance the potential pretentiousness of its themes. *Our Town* is the more successful of the two plays primarily because it offers a more convincing portrayal of the small events in life than *Skin* does and focuses attention more upon the life ritual itself than upon the idea of it. *Our Town* represents, therefore, a more successful embodiment of ideas in concrete action and characters drawn from actual life than *The Skin of Our Teeth* does, even though, like *Skin*, it is a theatricalist, stylized drama.

Wilder has stated in the preface to *Three Plays* that "*Our Town* is not offered as a picture of life in a New Hampshire village; or as a speculation about conditions of life after death (that element I merely took from Dante's *Purgatory*). It is an attempt to find a value above all price for the smallest events of our daily life. I have made the claim as preposterous as possible, for I have set the village against the largest dimensions of time and place. The recurrent words in this play (few have noticed it) are 'hundreds,' 'thousands,' and 'millions.' Emily's joys and griefs, her algebra lessons and her birthday presents—what are they when we consider all the billions of girls who have lived, who are living, and who will live?"

The action—which takes place in Grover's Corners, New Hampshire, on specific days in the years between 1901 and 1913—portrays both the routine daily life and the major events in the lives of George Gibbs and Emily Webb and their families. Each act centers about a scene of the family life which is preceded by a street scene involving the casual conversation of such characters as the milkman, the constable, and the paper boy—town folk in general. Act I consists of scenes showing a complete day in the town and in the Webb and Gibbs households when George and Emily are growing up. In acts II and III family scenes and the everyday street scenes are shown again but in relation, respectively, to the courtship and marriage of George and Emily and Emily's death.

But specific as the dates, places, and characters are—and Wilder provides all the important facts, including the history of the town, to individualize the action—it is immediately apparent that it is life rather than individual lives that is being enacted; that life is being presented rather than represented; and that the people, the place, and the time are the "All, the Everywhere and the Always." We are reminded, as we are in "The Happy Journey" and "Pullman Car Hiawatha," that this is a theatre play as the Stage Manager points to nonexistent properties which the audience is asked to imagine exist. And even as he is giving his detailed factual account of the town and its people, he violates the usual limitations of time sequence by using past, present, and future tenses concurrently; and Wilder achieves thereby on stage a present that encompasses all time—the action becomes an "Act in Eternity."

The Stage Manager presents the life on stage directly to the audience, addresses his comments about it to the audience, and at one point answers questions asked by actors planted in the audience. Like the property man in Chinese drama, he places the few properties on stage (which consist mainly of tables and chairs, ladders and planks); and, like the chorus in Greek theatre, he comments on the action, takes part in it himself, and functions as the author's mouthpiece. But in addition to his technical functions, he embodies the spirit of the town and selects and presents the scenes with a view to demonstrating the ideas behind them. For example, he announces in Act I that the play is to be a demonstration of how people grew up and married and lived and died "in the provinces north of New York at the beginning of the twentieth century," and he then offers scenes typical of the daily life in the Webb and Gibbs households. The metaphysical significance of the scenes is then expressed by George's sister Rebecca at the close of the act:

I never told you about that letter Jane Crofut got from her minister when she was sick. He wrote Jane a letter and on the envelope the address was like this: It said: Jane Crofut;

the Crofut Farm; Grover's Corners; Sutton County; New Hampshire; United States of America.

GEORGE: What's so funny about that?

REBECCA: But listen, it's not finished: the United States of America; Continent of North America; Western Hemisphere; the Earth; the Solar System; the Universe; the Mind of God—

This passage, prepared for by the previous presentation of actions specifically identifiable as to time and place but raised to the level of the eternal, anticipates the increasingly broadened scope of the action in acts II and III. Theatricalist technique by this means achieves a union of action and idea.

The vision Wilder offers of the human condition in *Our Town* is essentially tragic. It is a picture of the priceless value of even the most common and routine events in life and of the tragic waste of life through failure to realize the value of every moment. Unaware of the value of life, the people of Grover's Corners live their lives banally and seldom get beneath or above the surface of life. Yet even what they do realize and experience is beyond price; and this is the paradox that pervades the play and is the source of its tension. The conflict is basically inner, between consciousness and unconsciousness or between awareness and appreciation of life and insensibility and self-preoccupation.

The artistic problem basic to *Our Town* is that of showing that the events of life are at once not all they could be because they are taken for granted—but are priceless. Wilder meets this problem by repeating the quotidian scenes and viewing them and the central actions of each act (growing up, love and marriage, and death) from different perspectives of time and space and different metaphysical vantage points. By relating the ordinary events in the lives of these ordinary people to a metaphysical framework that broadens with each act, he is able to portray life as being at once significant and trivial, noble and absurd, miraculous and humdrum.

The ordinary characterizes all the scenes and narrative passages, and this quality is reinforced by colloquial dialogue liberally sprinkled with platitudes. The "facts" the Stage Manager recites about Grover's Corners are unstartling, commonplace, and statistical; and the answers he gives to questions asked by the actors in the audience (a woman concerned about the drinking in the town, a man indignant about the lack of awareness of social injustice and inequality, and a lady wondering about the cultural level of the town) indicate that the townspeople give little thought to such things. In Act II the Stage Manager-Minister repeats this idea when he says the weddings he has performed are interesting "once in a thousand times," and in Act III even death itself is shown to be a very commonplace, unstartling, and unfrightening event. Repetition of the quotidian scene, however, transforms the ordinariness into ritual; and, when the dead Emily returns to observe and relive her twelfth birthday in Act III, she becomes aware that the daily life of the town and of the families was humdrum and commonplace because taken for granted and not fully appreciated.

The real genius of *Our Town* consists in Wilder's success in making the ordinary interesting to watch and in portraying its intrinsic value without falling into bathos. Lacking the suspense that goes with a carefully plotted conflict between characters, the play admittedly draws heavily upon theatricalist novelty for fresh treatment of its materials; and much of its effect is owing to its appeal to audience nostalgia. But the material and the technical devices conceived for the benefit of the "group mind" have within them the seeds of a larger meaning; and this promise of a larger meaning gives suspense to the action. The people of Grover's Corners, being of the type Gertrude Stein called the "valley-born and the hill-bounded," exhibit the "localization in their thinking" that distinguishes them from their brethren living in flat country or on coastlines. Most of them never get very far from Grover's Corners during their lives; and most, like George and Emily, never care to. Their lack of interest in such abstractions as temperance, social equality, culture and beauty is characteristic of their kind. In contrast to the crusading Midwesterner George Brush of *Heaven's My Destination,* the significance of their lives lies concealed in their pattern of living in the trivia of "human nature" that they are steeped in. They do not try to find a concept in living as do Brush and Antrobus of *The Skin of Our Teeth.* Yet, the play says by implication that there is meaning even in lives in which there is no conscious and deeply felt guiding principle.

Each act has scenes (those involving such characters as the milkman, the constable, the paper boy) showing a simple bond of friendship among men and the routine family and community life. In Act I these scenes comprise the core of the action and represent the eternal rhythms of life; but in acts II and III they become objective correlatives for humanistic and theological perspectives. In Act II, the love and marriage of George and Emily symbolize the universal rite uniting nature's physical and spiritual forces; and, in Act III, Emily's death and brief return to life represent the apotheosis of life in its spiritual essence for which the speech by Rebecca at the close of Act I is a preparation. In addition, the scenes present an increasingly broad perspective of time and space. Act I, up to the time of the key passage by Rebecca, deals with the town in relation to its own history and geography; Act II, with the relationship between the wedding and the history and aspirations of Mankind in all ages; and Act III, with the relationship between life and eternity.

These relationships are expressed for the most part by the Stage Manager, either in his role as Stage Manager or as a character. In Act I, he gives the "facts" about the town; in Act II, he draws the parallel between physical nature and human nature and puts the wedding into the category of natural phenomenon. Both the earth and the people of Grover's Corners have grown older since Act I—three years before—but "Nature's been pushing and contriving in other ways, too: a number of young people fell in love and got married." Nature, he says, is interested in quantity—in propagation of the species—but there is something else in nature that is interested in quality. Just before the wedding he (as the Minister) says: "The real hero of this scene isn't on the stage at all, and you know who that is. It's like one of those European fellas said: every child born into the world is nature's attempt to make a perfect human being. Well, we've seen nature pushing and contriving for some time now. We all know that nature's interested in quality, too—that's why I'm in the ministry."

This humanistic affirmation of the dual—"higher" and "lower"—nature of men is given concrete, ironic enactment in the naive will to perfection expressed by Emily and George:

EMILY: I always expect a man to be perfect and I think he should be.
GEORGE: Oh . . . I don't think it's possible to be perfect, Emily.
EMILY: Well, my *father* is, and as far as I can see *your* father is. There's no reason on earth why you shouldn't be, too.
GEORGE: Well, I feel it's the other way around. That men aren't naturally good; but girls are.

The wedding, the central symbol of the fusion of nature's physical and spiritual purposes, puts those purposes and the will to perfection into a religious context. Yet the Stage Manager withholds judgment as to the value of the wedding: "I've married over two hundred couples in my day. Do I believe in it? I don't know." The cycle of life is filled as much with misery and pain as it is with happiness; and it always ends with death. The third act takes up this theme and presents it in action as the dead Emily, reluctant to quit life, observes her own funeral and begs to be allowed to relive one day of her life, her twelfth birthday, which the Stage Manager permits her to do. Having lost her life, she finds, while observing and taking part once more in daily events, that it is too great a gift for mortals to appreciate or understand. "Oh, earth," she cries, "you're too wonderful for anybody to realize you."

In this act, the Dead are seated on one side of the stage, while the funeral and scenes of daily life take place on the other. The intrusion of death here has been criticized as being inconsistent with the tone of the first two acts. John Mason Brown, for instance, felt it disappointing because the chill of death was "inescapable," its words were too colloquial, and its ideas too small. "The familiar aspects of living, dealt with so imaginatively in the first two acts, dwindle here into guesses unsupported by high imagination," Brown said. Emily's return was "touching," but the universality of the first two acts lost its "purity" in the third.[7]

It can be argued, however, that there would be a greater inconsistency if the words in the final act were less colloquial than they are in the first two. Although the chill of death is inescapable, it is precisely what brings the contrasting scenes of life to their highest emotional intensity. The action begins quietly in the cemetery and builds in intensity to Emily's climactic imprecation to her mother in the most moving lines in the play: "Oh, Mama, just look at me for one minute as though you really saw me. Mama, fourteen years have gone by. I'm dead. You're a grandmother, Mama. I married George Gibbs, Mama. Wally's dead, too. Mama, his appendix burst on a camping trip to North Conway. We felt just terrible about it—don't you remember? But, just for a moment now we're all together. Mama, just for a moment we're happy. Let's look at one another."

This moment is set against eternity; vibrant life, with all its joy and grief, happiness and suffering, is contrasted to passionless death. Emily can appreciate the value of life because she has lost it. From the vantage point of eternity she sees that it is largely wasted and that its tragedy lies in the failure of human beings to feel—as she does as she observes the scene of her twelfth birthday—the full intensity of each moment, good or bad, through the agency of consciousness, love. Her agonized realization of this sends her back to the Dead, where the moment and the human passions have no existence and are, therefore, not painful to contemplate.

Tragic waste, blindness and ignorance, failure to realize that even such a routine matter as greeting the milkman is a precious part of a priceless gift—that is the "discovery" the deceased Emily makes about life in Act III. But the presence of the Dead on stage with her has a mystical significance also. In contrast to Emily, who has just arrived among them, the Dead are indifferent to life on earth—or like Simon Stimson, whose life has been unhappy, contemptuous of it. While Stimson, Mrs. Soames, Mr. Carter, and Mrs. Gibbs still have their identity, the rest do not and will eventually lose it. The Stage Manager says of them at the opening of the act: "They're waitin' for something that they feel is comin'. Something important and great. Aren't they waitin' for the eternal part in them to come out clear?" All the problems and joys, the grief and happiness, and the love and indifference, it is suggested, are dissolved in the transcendent Whole: the perspective from which life is viewed in the last act is the "Mind of God."

A myth puts specific characters, actions, and themes into a microcosmic relationship with the universal forces that act upon and from within men; it draws together past and present; and it provides an analogy by which deep-felt needs, desires, aspirations, and fears of the individual become an expression of those of all men. The little New Hampshire town of Grover's Corners is Wilder's microcosm. His hero is human life itself; the universal forces acting upon it are Time, Nature, and Death; the forces acting from within it are Instinct, Love, Despair, and Apathy. Its scenes of daily life, love, marriage, and burial of the dead are the cyclical life-rituals of men in all times and places. The human condition is tragic because its hopes and aspirations and its customs and habits, which it feels are so important—as Emily and George feel their marriage is so important—are really not very important at all when considered in light of all the other human beings who experience the same things.

The lives of its people are tragic because in spite of unimportance they continue, as George and Emily have on their farm, in the belief that what they are doing is important; and their condition is tragic, finally, because the people of Grover's Corners never quite realize that because life is so short and because it is all they have, they should live every moment as intensely and consciously as their hearts will allow. A tragic vision requires the assumption that man is a potentially noble creature and that he lives his life in relation to some power, or "fate," or "destiny" that he is either at odds with or falls short of. Thus Oedipus struggles with the foreordained pattern set for his life by the gods, and Lear violates the moral law of order in the state by dividing up his kingdom. In *Our Town* the characters, while of humble circumstances, reach noble proportions as the beauty of their everyday lives is interwoven with their failure to realize its full potential; and the moral order of which they are a part and of which they fall short is one in which love is the highest law. This is the purport of

Emily's speech to her mother in Act III, when she begs Mrs. Webb to look at her as though she really saw her—with the consciousness that love engenders.

Regarded in the light of an assumed moral order of love, the presence of the Dead on stage in Act III receives added dramatic justification; for, while Wilder is not trying to show the "conditions of life after death," the Dead are, as the Stage Manager says, waiting for the "eternal part in them to come out clear"; and repetition of "Blessed Be the Tie That Binds," among other things, suggests that the moral order has a mystical basis. Moreover, the fact that Wilder borrowed the idea for the last act from Dante suggests that, like him, he intended his work to show that the love that animates and brings meaning to life is a manifestation of the cosmological order of things.

In this respect, T. S. Eliot's distinction between romantic and classical mysticism is apropos of *Our Town*. According to Elizabeth Drew, Eliot distinguishes between "romantic" and "classical" mysticism by noting that in romantic mysticism the tendency is to substitute divine love for human love. In Dante, whose mysticism was classical, the effort was "to enlarge the boundary of human love so as to make it a stage in the progess toward the divine."[8] Enlarging the scope of human love is Wilder's primary purpose in showing the disparity between the real value of life and the one of which the characters are aware. The audience does not feel any great concern for the outcome of the action since this is known from the beginning. It should feel, as Emily does, that failure to realize the value of life is essentially a failure to love every moment; and it should recognize that it is love which will be left after "the earth part burns away, burns out"—as the Stage Manager says of the Dead.

Our Town is thus a kind of religious festival—in accordance with Wilder's dramatic theory—celebrating Life. The Life it celebrates is the simplest and least pretentious imaginable; yet, as modestly as Wilder puts forth his view of life in *Our Town*, it has the depth and complexity and richness of a genuine tragic vision. He loves his people despite their shortcomings (perhaps, even, partly *because* of them) and clearly intends that the audience should too. In making the little

American town a mythical representation of civilized human life everywhere in all ages, he accomplished what he and Gertrude Stein conceived to be the main achievement of the literary masterpiece—the use of the materials of human nature to portray the eternal and universal residing in the collective "human mind." The theatricalist mode of presentation is so closely woven with the themes that it is an expression of them; and one feels compelled to say of *Our Town* what can be said of most great literary works: Its effects could not have been achieved by any other means.

III *The Matchmaker*

In his next play, Wilder turned theatricalism and farce into a satire about dramatic and social convention. *The Merchant of Yonkers* was a plea for a freer stage and a freer and fuller participation in life. Its first performance was at the Colonial Theatre in Boston on December 12, 1938, a little less than eleven months after the first production of *Our Town* at Princeton, New Jersey. On December 28, 1938, it opened in New York, where it had a short run of twenty-eight performances. It lay unused until Wilder revised it slightly, changed the title to *The Matchmaker*, and brought it out again in August, 1954, in Edinburgh. From Edinburgh it went to London, where it began a successful run the following November 4. In October, 1955, it was brought to Philadelphia, where it also succeeded; and when taken to New York, it engaged a run long enough to win "hit" status.

The Matchmaker doesn't differ materially from *The Merchant of Yonkers;* and it belongs, therefore, with the work of this earlier period of Wilder's career rather than with that after World War II. As Harold Clurman pointed out in his review of *The Matchmaker*, the failure of the earlier version and the success of the latter were probably owing to the difference in directors. *The Merchant* was directed by Max Reinhardt, for whom Wilder wrote it; and it failed, probably, because of what Clurman called the director's "unfamiliarity with American theatre custom."[9] *The Matchmaker* was directed by Tyrone Guthrie, who by common critical consent kept the action moving at the rapid pace it requires.

Wilder took much of the material for this play from Johann Nestroy's *Einen Jux will er sich Machen* (Vienna, 1842). He calls it a "free adaptation" of Nestroy's play, which was in turn based upon *A Day Well Spent* (London, 1835) by John Oxenham. "One way to shake off the nonsense of the nineteenth-century staging is to make fun of it," he wrote in the preface to *Three Plays*. "This play parodies the stock-company plays that I used to see at Ye Liberty Theatre, Oakland, California, when I was a boy." Much of its humor arises from the use of such old comic stage devices as mistaken identity, quick leaps for hiding places under tables, characters dressed in clothes of the opposite sex, and people caught in folding screens. It features stock characters and absurd situations that develop into a conventional complicated plot. It has a "villain," for instance, in the merchant Vandergelder, who tries to prevent the marriage of a young couple—his niece Ermengarde and the impecunious young artist Ambrose Kemper.

The action takes place in Yonkers during the 1880's and involves the efforts of the principal characters, whose enjoyment of life is in one way or another dependent upon Vandergelder, to "participate" in life. In addition to Ermengarde and Ambrose, the main characters include Vandergelder's two clerks, Cornelius and Barnaby, who go to New York in search of "adventure," and Dolly Levi, the "Matchmaker," who pretends to make a match for Vandergelder with a young, attractive woman (Irene Molloy) but actually makes it for herself. Vandergelder's "sensible" behavior and values are the obstacles in each instance to their free enjoyment of life, and the plot consists in the attempts of these people to combat his life-denying conventionality. His most formidable antagonist is Dolly Levi, who is the arranger, the artist of life who follows no doctrine except that of the full enjoyment of it and opposition to the conventional theories of "success" held by Vandergelder to whom work and money are life's highest values. She frankly and simply wants to marry him for his money, but her ideas about wealth are in direct opposition to his. She is determined to put Vandergelder's coins into circulation so they can free others from habit, convention, and isolation—for the enjoyment of life.

She explains her economic philosophy to Ambrose: "Money should circulate like rain water. It should be flowing down among the people, through dressmakers and restaurants and cabmen, setting up a little business here, and furnishing a good time there."

When she has conquered Vandergelder, his unconditional surrender contains assurances that his money will be spent instead of saved. Vandergelder is "sound" from the standpoint of conventional social values; for he has saved, worked hard, and been cautious. He is the stolid, pompous "self-made" man who equates the acquisition of riches and the exploitation of others with virtue and "good sense." The clever Dolly turns the platitudes he lives by to her own uses in such delicious bits of dialogue as the following:

> VANDERGELDER: Mrs. Molloy, I've got some advice to give you about your business.
> MRS. LEVI: Oh, advice from Mr. Vandergelder! The whole city should hear this.
> VANDERGELDER: In the first place, the aim of business is to make a profit.
> MRS. MOLLOY: Is that so?
> MRS. LEVI: I never heard it put so clearly before. Did you hear It?
> VANDERGELDER: You pay those girls of yours too much. You pay them as much as men. Girls like that enjoy their work. Wages, Mrs. Molloy, are paid to make people who do work they don't enjoy.
> MRS. LEVI: Mr. Vandergelder thinks so ably. And that's exactly the way his business is run up in Yonkers.

Enjoyment of life requires nurturing of a vice as well as the virtues. The ne'er-do-well Malachi expresses this bit of philosophy: "There are some people who say you shouldn't have any weaknesses at all—no vices. But if a man has no vices, he's in great danger of making vices out of his virtues, and there's a spectacle. We've all seen them: men who were monsters of philanthropy and women who were dragons of purity. We've seen people who told the truth, though the Heavens fall—and the Heavens fell. No, no—nurse one vice in your bosom. Give it the attention it deserves and let your virtues spring up modestly around it."

The clerks Cornelius and Barnaby are also in rebellion against Vandergelder and what he stands for. Yearning for excitement and resolving to go to New York for an "adventure," they blow up the tomato cans on the shelves of Vandergelder's store and leave. They are determined to have a good meal, to be "in danger," almost to get arrested, to spend all their money (three dollars), and to kiss a girl. Much of the best humor of the play consists in the attempts of these two—and, later, Irene Molloy—to have a part in the excitement of life heretofore denied them by conventions that equate "adventure" with foolishness. It is tender humor, a bit sentimental, even a bit "heartwarming," but nevertheless very enjoyable. The hilarious scene in Act III, where Dolly twists Vandergelder's exasperation with her into a hinted proposal, is one of Wilder's most comical.

It is interesting that while this play first appeared during the depression and featured a conflict between a villainous "boss" and his exploited employees, it was utterly unproletarian; it did not present a "problem" for which social amelioration or reform was needed. The play says in effect that Vandergelder is a moral rather than a social problem. Like *Heaven's My Destination*, it proposes that a vigorous, robust spirit of humanism is the answer to materialism: that effective reform should begin with the moral improvement of individuals rather than with legislation. But the play is really too good-natured to command serious consideration of its humanistic propositions; and perhaps this is one reason it failed in the thirties. Furthermore, it lacks the bite of real satire; and, while there is some ridicule aimed at conventional notions of "success," the character representing it, Vandergelder, is so candidly, absurdly, and farcically "bad" that the seriousness of what he represents does not become apparent.

There is less claim to serious attention and contemplation in this play than in any of Wilder's other full-length works; and it should be enjoyed for what it is—a farce. The laughter it evokes at Vandergelder and the conventions he embodies is that of compassion for a fellow human who is unaware of his own foolishness and not that of bitterness or contempt. Wilder often uses the phrase "makes fun of" where "satirizes" might ordinarily be expected. The difference in terminology is relevant, for he seldom *satirizes* in the sense that he holds persons up to ridicule or scorn. He takes the more gentle way of viewing his people with mild irony, and he achieves a kind of spontaneous gaiety out of his depictions of human folly instead of a laughter of superiority and contempt. The result in *The Matchmaker* is that one enjoys laughing at Vandergelder's absurdities but is not constrained to give much thought to their social or ethical significance.

IV *The Skin of Our Teeth*

In *The Skin of Our Teeth* (1942) Wilder brought his theatricalism and humanism together most successfully with the comic spirit. His literary passion in the late thirties and early forties was James Joyce, whom he was lecturing and writing about frequently,[10] and it was in *Finnegans Wake* that he found many of the materials he needed to reaffirm those traditional human values that had once again been lost sight of as Europe plunged into World War II. *Skin* was written, as he said, in his preface to *Three Plays,* "on the eve of our entrance into the war and under strong emotion and . . . it mostly comes alive under conditions of crisis."

The first audiences had difficulty understanding the play, or were impatient with it in spite of Tallulah Bankhead's hilarious enactment of Lily Sabina; and Harrison Smith reported in the *Saturday Review of Literature* that there were empty seats during the last act of the performance he saw. But most of the critics understood it—early reviews were generally favorable—and Wilder received his third Pulitzer Prize for it.

But when Henry Morton Robinson and Joseph Campbell, who were working on their "Key" to *Finnegans Wake,* saw the play, they immediately recognized its similarity to the Joyce novel. They published a series of articles in the *Saturday Review* titled "The Skin of Whose Teeth?" in which they showed that the play drew heavily upon *Wake* in themes, plot, characters, dialogue, and devices of presentation. They charged that the play was "an Americanized re-creation, thinly disguised," of *Finnegans Wake* and that the novel was "directly and frankly imitated, with but the flimsiest veneer to lend an American touch to the original features."[11]

Their evidence was indisputable, but many critics resented their insinuation that Wilder was guilty of plagiarism, and the argument that followed was nearly as fierce as the Michael Gold dispute twelve years before. George Jean Nathan, never favorable towards Wilder, not only applauded Campbell and Robinson but gave them his support.[12] Edmund Wilson, one of the few besides Wilder and Campbell and Robinson who understood Joyce's work at that time, wrote that while *The Skin of Our Teeth* deserved its success, it would no doubt suffer from comparison with *Finnegans Wake*.[13] Harrison Smith stated with some indignation that the question was not whether Wilder was a plagiarist, but whether he had "pulled a fast one on the public and especially those dramatic critics who received his play with mixed, but in some cases, wild enthusiasm."[14] *Time*, in spite of a generally unfavorable review of the play, maintained that Campbell and Robinson were "trying to make headlines out of footnotes, were confusing influences with imitations."[15] It quoted Wilder himself as saying that all he could do was suggest that those who were interested in the matter "read *Finnegans Wake* and make up their own minds."

Wilder has since acknowledged his debt to Joyce; and, except for Robinson, who renewed his charges and added others in an article in *Esquire* in March, 1957, the borrowing seems to have become accepted by critics as a legitimate use of one author's material by another for his own distinctive literary purposes. Where Wilder has borrowed, he has usually given credit to his sources; and he had used other sources besides Joyce in this play. For instance, he borrowed some of his ideas for comic stage effects (such as flying scenery) from Olsen and Johnson's slapstick *Hellzapoppin';* and, while it might be reasonable to expect an author to acknowledge one source, it is less reasonable to ask him to acknowledge two. Moreover, he might also be expected to give credits to his own earlier works such as "Pullman Car Hiawatha" and "The Long Christmas Dinner" from which he borrowed almost as heavily as he did from Joyce.

Although, as Wilder himself has said, the play is "profoundly indebted" to *Finnegans Wake,* Campbell and Robinson's charges are best forgotten; but their discoveries about the relationships between the novel and play can profitably be retained. Joyce, like other great authors, is likely to be borrowed from heavily for some time to come in spite of Campbell and Robinson's indignation; and it seems improbable that borrowing authors will always feel compelled to spell out the Joycean influence.[16]

Why Wilder found *Finnegans Wake* an agreeable source to borrow from is not difficult to understand, for much of its material and many of its themes were similar to those he had used in his own works prior to 1939, when Joyce's book appeared in its complete form. Wilder had already used a structure that showed the cyclical repetition of life through successive stages in "The Long Christmas Dinner" (1931). This structure and the historical theory it implied were similar to the circular structure of *Wake* and to Giambattista Vico's cyclical theory of history which Joyce himself borrowed from. In addition, nearly all of Wilder's works previous to 1939 reflected the same assumption of dualism and the mystical resolution of the conflict between opposites which Joyce achieved allegorically in *Wake* and borrowed from the renaissance Neo-Platonism of Giordano Bruno. Furthermore, Wilder had already employed the devices of amalgamating characters from myth, folklore, and religion and from literature and history in *The Cabala, The Bridge,* "Mozart and the Gray Steward," "The Flight into Egypt," and "Centaurs" for the purpose of demonstrating comparable cultural developments. And his own anthropological studies in Rome in the early twenties led him to much the same view about the similarity of human cultures that Joyce derived from Frazer's *The Golden Bough*—though it is quite likely that Wilder had read and been influenced by Frazer too. Undoubtedly *The Skin of Our Teeth* is deeply indebted to the Joyce work, but much of its technique and content also have precedent in Wilder's earlier works. Wilder can legitimately claim a good deal more in the play as his own than Campbell and Robinson allowed.

The three acts of *Skin* involve the struggles of Mankind to survive the periodic disasters that threaten it with extinction: glacial invasion, flood, and war. The first act pits Man against Nature; the second, Man against the moral order; and the third, Man against himself. The acts are arranged to encompass successively smaller units of time: Act I embraces geologic time; Act II, biblical time; and Act III, the time of recorded history. These units of time are focused upon the lives of the Antrobus family of Excelsior, New Jersey. The Antrobuses are the "typical American family," but they are also the Human Family; and, during the course of the play, they relive the whole history of the human race, its origin, its fight for survival against natural catastrophe, its fall and redemption, and its wars. In this representation the Antrobus family is like Joyce's Earwicker family, but with this difference: The Antrobuses, as Americans, are shown by Wilder to manifest their relationship (or at least their conviction that the relationship exists) to human destiny in their everyday lives. Joyce has Earwicker dream the events in *Finnegans Wake,* and the difference is an important one in that it points up the fact that Wilder was doing more than simply dramatizing the Joyce novel for American audiences: He was using some of Joyce's materials to implement his own mythical vision of the American family life as a microcosm and to bring the weight of past human experience and values to bear upon this age of perpetual crisis.

As in *Our Town,* the tone increases in seriousness with each act. In Act I, an Announcer—roughly the technical equivalent of the Stage Manager in *Our Town*—relates the news of the world as shown on lantern slides projected on a screen and declares that "The sun rose this morning at 6:32 a.m." The tone is comical, but this introductory scene relates the Antrobuses to present-day America, to biblical time, and to the Ice Age and prepares for the play within the play that follows. The play he introduces is repeatedly interrupted by characters stepping out of their roles and into others as actors: The actress who plays Sabina expresses her dissatisfaction with her role and with the play itself; actors become ill and have to be replaced by stage hands; the actor who plays Henry Antrobus has his own psychological problems and breaks down in the middle of a scene with Mr. Antrobus. In all these interruptions a Stage Manager appears from behind the curtain to try to keep the action moving. This comic theatricalism is abetted by such *Hellzapoppin'* burlesque antics as flying scenery and by the presence on stage of a dinosaur and a mammoth. Aside from its own comic effects, this material—understandable by the "greater number"—directs attention to the ideas behind the actions and the characters.

The characters are all allegorical figures on three levels: as Americans, as biblical figures, and as universal human types. Antrobus—the middle-class American, Adam, and the "father pilot" of the human race—has the general weaknesses and virtues of humanity in general of all times. The basic fact about him is that he does not change much from year to year or from one period of history to another; and his problems are also much the same in every age. He is always on the brink of a disaster caused either by natural forces outside him or by inner conflicts, but he manages to survive by the "skin of his teeth." His wife is at once the American mother, Eve, and the eternal mother. While Antrobus is at his best rational and needs reasons for survival, she acts from instinct and guards her family "like a tigress." She is anti-intellectual and narrow (". . . I'd burn ten Shakespeares to prevent a child of mine from having one cold in the head"); but in spite of humiliation by her philandering husband and the eternal wicked woman (Sabina) and of serious disaster she remains constant in her determination to save her family. She is both simple-minded and mysterious; and the force that makes her like a tigress appears to be instinct but is actually the secret of life itself. In Act II she throws a bottle with a letter in it into the ocean. In the letter, she says, "is written all the things a woman knows."

The two Antrobus children, Gladys and Henry, represent, respectively, Antrobus' hope for human perfection and proof that his hope can never be fully realized. Henry, who bears the red ochre emblem of Cain and is constantly at odds with the rest of the family, including Sabina, is the allegorical figure of evil. Antrobus' struggles with him represent enactment of the principle of dualism. Lily Sabina, the Antrobus maid, is also evil, but in a less fixed and absolute sense; for her sins are generally household or venial sins. She is the faint-hearted maid on the American-family level of the play;

but she also becomes, variously, the Semitic mythological figure of Lilith (the evil, wifely spirit); Miss Fairweather, to whom Antrobus turns when no disaster threatens and he doesn't need help and guidance; Sabina, the "robber of the Sabinerennen"—as told by Livy—whom Antrobus "raped . . . home" to insult Mrs. Antrobus, as she says in the free verse passage in Act I. Lily, who provides much of the comedy in the play, has all the weaknesses of her kind: lack of conviction; lack of courage before adversity; vanity; ignorance of everything above the level of appetite; prudishness; and self-righteousness.

These main characters are Americans who, like the people of *Our Town,* have hidden in their daily lives the key to the destiny of the human race. Antrobus' daily work at the office is a project of as great importance to him, it is implied, as the invention of the alphabet, the number system, and the wheel. When he pinches the maid, he commits a moral transgression which (though comical because of the discrepancy) is parallel to the rape of the Sabines by the men of Romulus. When his wife tells their daughter Gladys to pull down her skirt, she is preserving the morals of the race; but, when Antrobus kisses the bathing beauty, he is corrupting them.

Conflict in the play is dialectical; for ideas are pitted against one another in opposite pairs. Antrobus himself does not change; only his ideas do. The comic-serious tone increases tension between the ideas with irony. As time-present and time-past are put into the eternal present, the action and characters attain the allegorical level. Lily Sabina stands in dialectical opposition to Mrs. Antrobus, Henry-Cain to Antrobus, and, again, Henry-Cain to Gladys. In opposition to all of them in Act I is the glacier, which represents natural disaster—a phenomenon for which no cause is indicated; it unites the human family, good and bad, in the common cause of survival. The unity and the determination to survive, however, come only after Antrobus decides that the race is worth saving. He undergoes an inner struggle of doubt and despair when Mrs. Antrobus refuses to give shelter to Homer and Moses and when he sees his own evil in Cain. His decision to survive comes when Moses and Homer (Judge and Professor, Hebraism and Hellenism, Sweetness and Light) are saved and when Gladys announces that in school she had an "A" in "Conduct" and had recited perfectly in assembly (again, sweetness and light).

The humanistic affirmation of the play is clear enough, and again Wilder's humanism ends in faith. The act ends with Gladys' reciting the opening lines of Genesis and with Sabina's calling to the audience to help save the human race. The dramaturgy, then, is theatricalist and presentational, the thematic treatment allegorical, the themes religious-humanistic. The question remains, however, as to whether form, style, and themes come together in a successful fusion.

Act I shows survival to be a matter of will and courage based upon faith in human and religious values, but Act II depicts it as a matter of acceptance of moral responsibility. The allegory is more directly religious than in Act I, for it affirms the principle of individual responsibility in Old Testament terms. In Act II geologic, biblical, and modern times are telescoped again, as they are in Act I, with an Atlantic City convention which is shown concurrently as an ordinary businessmen's convention; as a convention of the "Ancient and Honorable Order of Mammals, Subdivision Humans"; and as the biblical world just before the Flood. The convention is a sort of combined Sodom and Gomorrah and Vanity Fair where pleasure and irresponsibility run rampant. The end inevitably is destruction, either through the self-destructive nature of its pleasure-seeking or by a God of Justice.

The central symbols of the act are the bingo parlor and the fortune teller which signify, respectively, chance and destiny, or circumstance and fate, or accident and predestination. The right (moral) choice, it is implied, reduces the extent to which chance, accident, or circumstance governs life. The Conveeners have their "chance" to abandon their pleasure-seeking and choose the right way, but they fail. Antrobus, who nearly fails, is saved only at the moment of the Flood when he leaves Lily Sabina-Fairweather behind and accepts his responsibilities to his "family"—Mankind. Absent from this act are the humanistic-allegorical figures of Act I—Homer, Moses, the Muses. The moral content of Act II is in a primarily religious context—Judaic-Christian in its emphasis upon retribution and redemption and, of course, its basis in Genesis. The vision in Act II is one of man paying heavily for his moral transgressions and follies. Torn between his responsibilities to his family and his desire for the easier life of indulgence, Antrobus wavers but redeems himself at the last moment; but his fellows at the convention, refusing to heed the warning of the apocalyptic Fortune Teller, follow the course of pleasure and die for it.

Act III resumes the religious-ethical themes of the first two acts and shows Antrobus courageously rebuilding after war. He still has Sabina and Cain to contend with and is weary and discouraged; but he again makes the decision to accept his responsibility to the human family. Once more, his guidance and justification are in his books—Spinoza, Plato, Aristotle, and the Bible. His attitude is one of resignation but hope:

> Oh, I've never forgotten for long at a time that living is struggle. I know that every good and excellent thing in the world stands on the razor-edge of danger and must be fought for—whether it's a field, or a home, or a country. All I ask is the chance to build new worlds and God has always given us that. And has given us
>
> (*Opening the book*)
>
> voices to guide us; and the memory of our mistakes to warn us. Maggie, you and I will remember in peacetime all the resolves that were so clear to us in the days of war. We've come a long ways. We've learned. We're learning. And the steps of our journey are marked for us here.

The play does not imply that the world should adopt American ideals and mores. What it says is that hidden in American life are the weaknesses that have hindered and the moral and religious values that have assured man's survival since the beginning of civilization. Wilder's historical view here rejects the theory of progress; for the circular form, with Lily Sabina repeating her opening lines at the very end of the play, indicates that history will follow a similar cycle. But Antrobus is not the hopeless prey of endless cycles of disaster; he says: "We've come a long ways. We've learned. We're learning." He can do nothing about natural disasters, and evil (Cain) is so much a part of him that he knows he can't escape it; but he can and does keep evil under control; and, with courage and acceptance of moral responsibility, he can eliminate disasters which are of his own making. With faith in his better self—as defined in the great works of his cultural heritage—and in God, he will continue to survive and even to triumph although other creatures perish.

This message is the serious side of *The Skin of Our Teeth;* but Wilder's humanistic temperament sees a comical, ridiculous facet of the good and bad in men—and in the American—as well as a serious one. The other side of the good Mrs. Antrobus is the prudish one. The other side of Adam-Antrobus is the vulgarian who makes his entrance in Act I with: "I'll be scalded and tarred if a man can't get a little welcome when he comes home. Well, Maggie, you old gunny-sack, how's the broken down old weather hen?—Sabina, old fishbait, old skunkpot.—And the children,—how've the little smellers been?" The theatricalism—which is both comic and serious in intent—is intended in part to offset the didacticism and conventionalism of the themes. But it sometimes does its job too well, for it tends to overwhelm the themes. Moreover, the mixture of comedy and seriousness does not always come off successfully. One might ask, for example, how the author can have his Fortune Teller tell about "shameful things" and "total destruction" one minute and expect his audience to take those warnings seriously in light of the comic handling of Antrobus' seduction by Sabina which follows.

Furthermore, the play lacks the effective objective correlative that *Our Town* has in its repeated view of the ordinary life of the town, and it also does not have the compelling concrete demonstration of its propositions of the other play. By Act II of *Our Town* Emily and George, in spite of the fact that they are generalized, are powerful emotional referents; in *Skin* the referents are weak because they are abstractions from the beginning; and their actions lack, therefore, the basis in common experience that gives concreteness to the themes of *Our Town*. The humanistic theme of sweetness and light in the first act, for example, which is demonstrated by Gladys' announcement that her conduct and performance at school were "perfect," is intended to illustrate the operation of those great human values in everyday American life and to indicate their importance by making them the deciding factor in Antrobus' decision to fight for survival; but the actual effect of this demonstration of the great by the small is to reduce the former without raising the latter to the point of convincing affirmation.

The same result also comes of having the Muses, Homer, and Moses (who are "typical New York out-of-works") join in singing "Tenting Tonight." The effect is not, as intended, to raise the American camp meeting to an affirmative humanistic level, but to make comical the humanistic symbols used seriously in Act III. Again, in Act II the moral degradation of Antrobus is handled with such lightness of tone that the "shame" of it is not convincing—it looks more like a minor indiscretion than a threat to the moral fiber of the human race. In Act III, the moral weakness of Sabina and the "evil" of Cain are confronted by Antrobus, who admits his own evil and moral weakness but affirms his survival again on the basis of values he has inherited and maintained. These values, which can be identified generally as the search for ideal truth and beauty (Spinoza), moral order and responsibility (Plato), belief in the potential divinity of man (Aristotle), and faith in God (Genesis again) are intended to be taken with full seriousness in Act III. But, after the almost cavalier treatment of the Antrobus affair with Sabina in Act II, the recitations of passages from the philosophers in Act III seem almost objectionably serious.

The Skin of Our Teeth is Wilder's most complete and direct expression of his theory of the relationship between the American and "destiny," as well as the most complete achievement of his theatricalist theories. If the play proves anything, it is that theatricalism and allegory can be a dangerous mixture unless leavened with some degree of concrete fact: they must have some basis in real experience. Literal and allegorical meanings, comedy and seriousness, theatricalism and realism (almost totally lacking) are inadequately balanced to make the themes convincing and provide a unified vision of a faltering, absurd but noble mankind surviving not only because of but in spite of itself. *Our Town* is sufficient proof, therefore, that Wilder's thematic purposes are best served by the presence of at least enough slice-of-life presentation to put his themes in direct relation with objective experience.

Perhaps it is not possible to do successfully what Wilder undertook to do in *The Skin of Our Teeth*—to relate a single family to the "All, the Everywhere, and the Always"—without making the family convincing first in concrete, partly realistic terms. To do so, as he does in *Our Town*, is a more effective method of drawing the audience into the action in order—in ritual or festival fashion—to formalize its deepest ethical and religious convictions. The theme of the play is really less optimistic than the comedy and theatricalism lead one to believe; for the play says at one level that there is little we have ever been able to do about periodic catastrophes except to cling to our best spiritual achievements and faith in God. There are a good many laughs in *The Skin of Our Teeth*, which may very well be the best thoroughly theatricalist work of the American theatre;[17] but it seems to demonstrate also that religious humanism and burlesque are not very compatible dramatic ingredients.

Yet one hesitates to try to say anything final about *Skin*. Time has been good to it, and it seems likely to outlive many better made plays. Wilder's statement that it comes to life best during times of crisis probably accounts for its great success in Germany and Poland since World War II. It is basically a tribute to man's indomitable will and an expression of faith; and if, in a day of perpetual crisis, it can give expression to and help to achieve the kind of faith it demonstrates—particularly in Act III—it will have fulfilled one of the highest functions of literary art.

CHAPTER 5

Existentialism and Humanism

IN 1942, the year *The Skin of Our Teeth* was first produced, Wilder enlisted in the Intelligence Corps of the Air Force as a captain and spent the next three years in the United States, North Africa, and Italy; he was discharged in 1945 as a lieutenant-colonel. As an intelligence officer his special concern in the battle against dictators was with information and resistance from within enemy territory—a fact which probably turned his thoughts to the subject of absolute power and freedom. It is also likely that the Mediterranean atmosphere drew his mind to the classic instance of absolute power and civil resistance to it that culminated in the assassination of Julius Caesar in Rome on March 15, 44 B.C. In addition, the loss of a friend, Roman poet Lauro De Bosis, who was killed while attempting to organize a resistance movement against Mussolini, made the fact of resistance and the question of living and dying for principles a personal one. These factors, plus an interest in the philosophy of crisis that had come out of the resistance movement in France, seem to have been the main causes of the writing of *The Ides of March*, one of the best American novels of the post-World War II period.

I *The Ides of March*

Absolute power and resistance to it in Caesar's Rome is the subject matter of *The Ides of March*, but Wilder's purpose is not simply to retell the history of Caesar's overthrow by the Roman aristocracy in order to draw parallels with events during World War II. His Caesar has almost nothing in common with Mussolini or with Hitler except that he is a dic-

tator. Unlike the fascist dictators, he is a hero who holds
Rome under his command because he is resolute and decisive and because, unlike his antagonists, he is wholly committed to action. He is the most powerful man in the world
because he has put aside all illusions about universal meaning and benevolence, turned to advantage the isolation which
is the condition of all men, and responded decisively to all
situations demanding decision. A man of responsibility, Caesar
contrasts to his arch-antagonist Brutus, who, guided by ideals
and systems of philosophy, is irresolute, irresponsible, and
weak. *The Ides of March* is, therefore, an ironic turnabout
on the subject of absolute power and freedom; for it is the
dictator Caesar who, being free, stands as a symbol of the
greatness, nobility, and power of the man who has discovered
his humanity through both the suffering and the triumph of
total "engagement." The fall of such a man is tragic, and
Wilder's Caesar attains real tragic stature.

Wilder's interest in the existentialist philosophy of Sartre
after World War II can be readily explained. A humanist like
Sartre, Wilder had always maintained the position that ethics
have to be defined in an exclusively human context without
reference to religious or philosophical preconceptions. Although his humanism, unlike Sartre's, ended in religious faith,
he was careful to keep moral considerations separate from
religious doctrine and insist, as Sartre did, that any meaningful prescription for human conduct has to be grounded in
experience rather than *a priori* philosophical or religious
ideas. This view was implicit in *The Bridge,* for instance,
where he maintained that any meaning that life was to have
would have to come from individuals themselves and that
the first step in the creation of a meaningful existence was
commitment with love to responsibility for others. His interest
in Sartre's philosophy—which led him in 1948 to adapt Sartre's
Morts sans sépulture (*The Victors*) for the American stage—
was that of a believer and a moralist in the affirmations of a
non-believer. His Caesar is the embodiment of the Sartre hero;
and Caesar's tragedy is in part the inevitable tragedy of such
a character.

In his "Existentialism and Humanism," Sartre declared that
among the major tenets of existentialism are the propositions

that existence precedes essence, that man is "nothing else but that which he makes of himself," that he is responsible for all his fellowmen, that he is "condemned to be free," that there is no reality or morality except in commitment to action, and that there are no *a priori* values. Therefore, the "moral choice is comparable to the construction of a work of art"; for, like the artist, man is forced to create his own moral world.[1]

Wilder's Caesar has become and remained ruler of Rome because he has acted in accordance with these assumptions. His loneliness as ruler of Rome represents man's isolation in the universe and in the world. But that isolation gives him heroic potential. Having directed the fortunes of Rome from war to peace, he now wants to build a greater Rome; but he must first answer the question of what its purpose will be. Since he rules Rome and since it rules the world, he, in effect, directs the destiny of the world, is responsible for all his fellowmen, and is charged with defining the purpose of life. He writes to his friend Turrinus: "The projects which now visit me . . . involve certain elements about which I am not certain that I am certain. To put them into effect I must be clear in my mind as to what are the aims in life of the average man and what are the capabilities of the human being. Man—what is that? What do we know of him? His Gods, liberty, mind, love, destiny, death—what do these mean?"

Committed to life and "the obligations of living," he is impatient with philosophy. "I have regarded philosophy with impatience," he tells Turrinus in a letter, "as a tempting but fruitless exercise of the mind and as a flight from the obligations of immediate living." His own experience has convinced him that any ethical position must be based upon response to situations that demand vital decisions—upon what Sartre calls "engagement." He says: "The first and last schoolmaster of life is living and committing oneself unreservedly and dangerously to living; to men who know this an Aristotle and a Plato have much to say; but those who have imposed cautions upon themselves and petrified themselves in a system of ideas, them the masters themselves will lead into error.

Brutus and Cato repeat liberty, liberty, and live to impose on others a liberty they have not accorded to themselves——." There can be no freedom, he maintains, except in responsible action; in the acceptance of the necessity of making a moral choice for which the individual alone is responsible and which in its enactment affects his fellowmen. Responsibility is the highest morality; and the actress Cytheris observes of Caesar that he is essentially a teacher and that "the essence of what he has to teach is moral, is responsibility."

His ethical conviction that man is compelled to be free and that "Life has no meaning save that which we may confer upon it" derives from his metaphysical belief that man is alone in a universe that does not know he exists—a world Sartre held to be meaningless. But while he is quite sure it is meaningless, he is not certain; and he is constrained from issuing an edict he has written abolishing religion because an element of doubt remains in his mind. "Some last hesitation arrests my hand," he tells Turrinus; and, unable to commit his conviction to action, he remains in doubt.

Caesar is thus a counterpart of the man of faith. Where the believer's faith is troubled by doubt, Caesar's disbelief is qualified by uncertainty. He is unable to make a final statement about the absence of any "mind behind our existence" because of the possibility of mystery in four realms of his life and in life generally: love, great poetry, his epilepsy, and his position as leader of Rome. "If I acknowledge the possibility of one such mystery," he says, "all the other mysteries come flooding back." These realms offer possibilities of mystery because they are paradoxical: they may spring from the lowest in man's nature, but Caesar has observed or felt in them the highest human experiences. For example, love may be an instinct, as it is in Clodia Pulcher; or it may be a passion in which the self is forgotten, as it is with Catullus. The great lyrics Catullus writes for Clodia may spring alike from love and hatred, good and evil. Caesar's epilepsy may be simply a physical disorder, yet during his seizures he has a vision in which he seems to "grasp the fair harmony of the world." And, finally, he observes that while he has attempted, perhaps from wholly selfish reasons, to shape Rome to his idea and "give it a sense," he is not entirely sure that he is not actually an instrument of destiny.

Suggested in these mysteries is a teleological option to the existentialist assumption that the universe is without meaning; that is, the possibility that while the initial causes of love, great poetry, his epilepsy, and his power may be easily enough explained in human terms, the final causes may reside in a meaningful, ordered universe—in God. The metaphysical irony basic to *The Ides of March* consists in Wilder's substitution of "Unknowable" for Sartre's "meaningless" in describing the operation of the universe. Wilder presents a very convincing portrayal in Caesar of the existentialist ethical and metaphysical assumptions of Sartre; but he then undermines the certainty behind those assumptions by affirming the presence of mystery, which compels a tentative attitude towards them. The recognition that life is essentially a mystery sets into motion Caesar's inquiries into the meaning and nature of life; and the applicability is clear from the epigraph Wilder chose from a passage in *Faust* and glossed as "Out of man's recognition in fear and awe that there is an Unknowable comes all that is best in the explorations of his mind,— even though that recognition is often misled into superstition, enslavement, and overconfidence."

This statement is in general the philosophical basis of the book. But while *The Ides of March* is a philosophical novel, it is a *novel* and not a work of philosophy. Its philosophical framework is grounded in the lives—both inner and outer— of the characters; and, considering the difficulties inherent in the imaginary-document mode of presentation Wilder uses, the characters are remarkably individual and alive. The thematic tensions that derive from the conflicts in Caesar's mind and grow between him and his antagonists include those of belief and disbelief, necessity and choice, tyranny and benevolence, and freedom and responsibility.

These tensions are related by means of three types of documents that convey the life of Rome and Caesar's ethical ideas and metaphysical speculations. The first type includes letters, reports, directives, and pamphlets which are of direct and immediate interest and which convey the flux of Roman life. These documents provide the action of the narrative; for they have the conflict, tension, and immediacy of scenic presentation. They generally lack reflection and summary for they are official papers, orders by Caesar, or incitements to action against him; the letters provide a kind of dialogue of action between such correspondents as Brutus and Servilia, Clodia and Catullus, and Caesar and Cleopatra.

The second type of document functions technically as summary narration which tells what has happened and perhaps conjectures about what will happen. These documents, like the first type, describe the major characters and relate their actions; but, in contrast to the first, the writers usually offer their own comments about the events and the people they write about and the authors are themselves minor characters who are only marginally involved in the main course of events. Examples of this type are the passages from the Commonplace Book of Cornelius Nepos and the letters of his wife Alina to her sister; in these such incidents as Cleopatra's arrival in Rome and Catullus' death are related.

The third type of document is primarily reflective in nature. Most of the documents in this group consist of Caesar's letters to Turrinus, but they also include Cytheris' letters to Turrinus. These epistles contain most of the ethical and religious comment in the book, and they reveal Caesar not only as the private man and student of life but also as the ruler. The sources of reflection in these letters are for the most part the incidents reported in the documents of the first type; and, while these letters tend to be essayistic, they avoid the kind of essayism so objectionable to Jamesian critics— where the author speaks as author—because they are written by characters who are steeped in the life they comment on and reveal themselves as they write.

All these documents are arranged into four chapters organized according to theme and time; and each succeeding chapter embraces and extends the previous one. Each ends with a misfortune for Caesar—a foreshadowing of the final disaster of March 15. The first begins with a report to Caesar by the College of Augurs about the behavior of the birds of prophecy, and it ends with Caesar's epileptic seizure after the first assassination attempt and during Clodia Pulcher's party; it covers the month of September, 45 B.C. The second chapter opens with a letter, dated August 17, from Servilia to Pompeia about the expected arrival of Cleopatra, and it ends with the incident in which Antony and Cleopatra are found in an embrace. The third begins with Caesar's letter of August 9 to the president of the College of the Vestal Virgins requesting purification of the rituals, and it ends with the profanation of the rites by Claudius Pulcher and with Caesar's divorce from Pompeia because of her part in it. And the final chapter opens with Servilia's letter, dated August 8, to Brutus asking him to return to Rome to help depose Caesar; and it ends with the assassination. With each of the first three chapters ending badly for Caesar, the feeling of inevitability is established.

The vision Wilder achieves is one in which the people of Rome have a direct relation with human destiny. Since Caesar's fate is known in advance, attention is focused from the beginning upon the question of its causes—a strategy (similar to that of *The Bridge of San Luis Rey*) which compels the reader to give close attention to the details of character and action in order to find the reasons for the disaster. The question that commands the reader's interest is: "What sort of person is Caesar and what factors in his own personality and in the personalities of the people of Rome brought about his assassination?"

The most palpable factor in Caesar is the self-destroying nature of his belief in total commitment to action. Having achieved freedom for himself through the responsibility gained by "engagement," he has forgotten that others—also "condemned to be free"—will seek to test their freedom through decisive commitments to action. Furthermore, deprived of the responsibility Caesar has assumed, they will commit themselves to irresponsible acts. Thus Catullus launches an irresponsible campaign against him; and Brutus, not really understanding freedom, assassinates Caesar in its name. The actress Cytheris says of Caesar: "It is not that, like other tyrants, he is chary of according liberty to others; it is that, loftily free himself, he has lost all touch with the way freedom operates and is developed in others; always mistaken, he accords too little or he accords too much." He has forgotten that other men have to explore the limits of liberty before they can assume responsibility. Ironically, he has so shaped Rome to his own idea, that, when he falls, his Rome must tumble also.

Another factor in Caesar that leads to his downfall is his isolation as a ruler. Much of the sympathy the reader feels for him arises from awareness of the discrepancy between the private Caesar—who shows real compassion and solicitude for his invalid friend Turrinus, tolerance and concern for Catullus, and grief for his dead daughter—and the public one who refuses to permit Cleopatra to bring their child to Rome. The discrepancy between the two Caesars is the paradoxical result of his conviction, on the one hand, that because man is alone in the universe he must act under that assumption and of his personal inclination, on the other hand, to dispel his loneliness with acts of love and kindness. "The condition of leadership adds new degrees of solitariness to the basic solitude of mankind," he tells Cleopatra.

Her reply indicates her awareness of the extent to which his isolation as ruler is self-imposed and excessive: "You have described to me the solitude of a ruler. A ruler has reason to feel that most of the approaches made to him are colored with self-interest. Is it not the danger of rulers to increase this solitude by ascribing to others that motivation alone? I can imagine a ruler turned to stone by such a view of his fellow men and turning to stone all those who approach him." She adds that ". . . you have, indeed, created for yourself a solitude that is excessive even for the ruler of the world."

The fact that metaphysical and ethical necessity in part governs the public Caesar but that he himself has chosen to accept isolation and responsibility establishes him as a tragic representation of the human condition. In living by the laws of the universe, he represents the condition of man; and, because he *chose* to do so, he is tragic. But the real essence of his tragedy is his excess in both isolation and responsibility, which has detached him from the aristocracy and generated contempt on his part and hostility on theirs. Caesar the dictator is respected but not loved; for his physician Sosthenes says of him: "Caesar does not love, nor does he inspire love.

He diffuses an equable glow of ordered good will, a passion-less energy that creates without fever, and which expends itself without self-examination or self-doubt."

The private Caesar, whom these people never know, is revealed primarily in his letters to Turrinus; and in the con-trast between what the public Caesar has to be and what the private Caesar is lies the irony that evokes a feeling of in-evitability and of pathos at his death. While the letters to Turrinus contain Caesar's metaphysical and ethical reflections, they also reveal his emotional depth. His urbane and sophisti-cated style and his loftiness of thought are softened by feelings that are unexpressed but grounded in the tone of the letters. Turrinus, having lost his arms and legs in war, lives in se-clusion on Capri. He is a sufferer, to Caesar a fellow-sufferer, whom he respects because Turrinus has been schooled in affliction and has gained from it a wisdom and courage non-sufferers lack. The letters to him are characterized by warmth and complete confidence, and they reflect Caesar's innermost feelings and thoughts. They convey, therefore, the various facets of his character: the reflective Caesar; the Caesar whose love for Rome is deeper than his love for its citizens; the Caesar—reminiscent of Shaw's—who is amused at the follies of men (and particularly by the religious follies of the women of Rome and the calculating ambition of Cleopatra); and the angry and disgusted ruler who is contemptuous of the motives and principles of his fellow Romans. Yet withal they reveal a man of dignity and nobility, of great understanding and sympathy for those whom life has hurt. Drawn with-out sentimentality, he is a powerful figure; and by the end of the book he has gained the full stature of a tragic pro-tagonist. He is Wilder's most complex and convincing char-acter.

Of the other characters in the book, the women emerge most clearly and effectively and make the greatest impact upon the life of Rome and upon Caesar. Except for Caesar none of the men is delineated sharply. Cicero's letters tell more about Caesar than about Cicero, and Catullus' letters reveal more about Clodia than himself. But the letters of the women define distinctly and often ironically the personalities of their writers. Deeply involved in matters of everyday life, these women have a tremendous influence upon the fortunes of Rome through their power over the men. The notorious Clodia Pulcher incites Claudius Pulcher to profane the rites of the Good Goddess; and she inspires Catullus' great lyrics to "Lesbia," poems that move Caesar so profoundly that he is constrained to call great poetry one of the real mysteries in life and to observe that Catullus' strange, unrequited passion for Clodia is an instance of the mystery that is love. Servilia pens the letter that first puts the idea of resistance into Brutus' mind—she is the woman whom Caesar has given in younger days "the rose-colored pearl that she wears so religiously at every celebration of the Founding of the city." And from the Queen of Egypt—passionate, impulsive, capricious, loving a Caesar who comprehends her better than she knows herself and loving him because Egypt's welfare depends upon him—come the letters and the state documents showing her in all her phases: the offended mother, the proud queen carrying the dignity of a nation and a dynasty with her, the playful mistress, and the distressed and misunderstood one.

Influencing consciously or unconsciously the men and institutions of Rome, these women act upon their own feelings and intuitions rather than upon reflection; and their power is that of emotions rather than of intellect. Practical above all and steeped in the trivia of everyday, they have great spiritual potential which could be realized, as Caesar observes, if directed into useful human activity instead of into such absurdities as primitive religious rites. "Let each woman find out in herself her own Goddess," he tells Turrinus and expresses what religious ritual should mean. Yet the women are generally more effectual than the men because, like Caesar, they commit themselves to action.

The document mode of presentation permits Wilder to get both inside and outside his characters without the "editorial presence" of an omniscient author. The characters define themselves by what they say and do or are reported to have said and done; and from the interplay of conflicting sentiments, viewpoints, and reports about a number of subjects and actions arises a vision that has the complexity, intensity, and paradoxes of life itself. With this method the danger of the philosophical novel is avoided, for the life presented is not merely a contrivance to illustrate ideas but has immediacy. While Caesar in general embodies the free man in existentialist terms, his part is not unnatural to him in his capacity as a leader. Moreover, existentialism by its nature precludes fitting life to a scheme of ideas; for it requires instead that action rather than ideas be the source of reflection.

The Ides of March is Wilder's best novel to date, for complexity of vision and intricacy of organization place it well above his other four novels. Although not likely to be so widely read as *The Bridge,* it is a better book in terms of craftsmanship and character development. While *The Bridge* has a number of well-developed characters, none has the intellectual and emotional completeness of Caesar, who has all the dimensions of a great tragic protagonist. Although the documentary method precludes the dramatic effect of direct presentation of incidents ("scenic" presentation), it makes up for this loss by enabling the author to convey objectively not only his characters' minds but their actions. In the intricate picture he presents of the interplay between the outer and inner lives of these characters, Wilder achieves the most completely satisfying vision presented in his works of fiction so far.

II *The Alcestiad*

Like *The Matchmaker, The Alcestiad* has its premiere performance in Edinburgh, where it was presented in 1955 under the title *A Life in the Sun*—a title imposed upon it by the producer and one with which Wilder was not happy. It failed in Edinburgh; but subsequent performances in Switzerland, Austria, and Germany achieved notable critical and popular success. Whether or not Wilder intends to bring the play to the United States for a major run remains to be seen; but at present, since he is having a musical score written, it is possible that American audiences will see it as an opera.

The legend of Alcestis and her sacrifice interested Wilder for some time before he wrote *The Alcestiad.* In *The Woman of Andros,* the hetaira Chrysis, while reflecting about "why we suffer," had observed that the answer would come some day when "I shall be among the shades underground and some wonderful hand, some Alcestis, will touch me and will show me the meaning of all these things. . . ." In this novel the hoped-for Alcestis was Christ, whose birth brought religious sanction to the moral and ethical principles Chrysis and Pamphilus already embraced.

Wilder also related the moral to the religious in the Alcestis legend in *The Ides of March* when he had Catullus recite the "Lost Alcestiad of Catullus"—Wilder's own version—at the Pulcher party just after the first attempt to assassinate Caesar; and this narrative is the basis for Act I of *The Alcestiad* in which it brings a religious dimension to the legend by having Alcestis seek to renounce life in order to serve Apollo. Wilder not only added it to the main incidents of the great Greek original by Euripides but also added a third act and a satyr-play to give religious and metaphysical meanings to the action. The result was an allegory in which self-sacrifice is viewed in its ethical, religious, and metaphysical implications.

The Alcestiad retains, however, much of the flavor of Greek drama. Constructed like a Greek tetralogy, it has three serious parts and the satyr-play. It also has in the Watchman a chorus, for he has the role of the Stage Manager in *Our Town* in that he interprets the action, relates antecedent events, and reports the consequences and effects of the action upon the citizens in general. Although the second act includes the major incidents—Alcestis' sacrifice for Admetus and her resurrection by Hercules—of the Greek original, Wilder, as he usually does when he borrows, alters the structure, myth, and characters to suit his own purposes. For one thing, *The Alcestiad* covers the thirty years from Alcestis' marriage to Admetus to her death; and the first act occurs on a day ten years prior to the action of the *Alcestis* and the third act takes place twenty years after her death and resurrection. For another, Wilder changes Admetus from the coward of the Euripides version to a beloved king and husband who is unafraid of death, who enjoys the blessings of divine grace, and who is not unworthy of Alcestis' sacrifice. And Wilder's Alcestis and Hercules, unlike their forerunners in *Alcestis*, consciously try to find meaning in their lives.

In maintaining the characters, the setting, and the main incident of the original Greek version, Wilder follows the way of Cocteau (*The Infernal Machine*) and Sartre (*The Flies*) rather than that of T. S. Eliot, who so transformed the Alcestis legend in *The Cocktail Party* that he had to point out the relationship. Wilder's reason is clear and simple: The Greek myth in its own dress gave him—as the Oedipus myth and the *Oresteia* gave Cocteau and Sartre—the materials to put his characters in direct relationship with the gods; that is, the laws of the universe. That relationship, as Wilder depicts it, is quite different from the relationships shown by Cocteau and Sartre, whose gods are either malicious or alien towards men and whose protagonists gain humanity through suffering at their hands or freedom through rebellion against them. The picture Wilder offers is, however, of a God of love (Apollo) who tries to make himself felt and understood by men but is unable to do so without human help. Wilder's mankind is helpless before circumstance until shown the way to humanity—and thence to divinity—by one who commits herself wholly to the highest expression of love—self-sacrifice.

The Alcestiad is an existentialist allegory portraying the mystic's pilgrimage. It presents directly the religious affirmation that was only suggested as an option to Caesar's skepticism in *The Ides of March*. Wilder himself has said: "On one level my play recounts the life of a woman—of many women— from bewildered bride to sorely tested wife to overburdened old age. On another level it is a wildly romantic story of gods and men, of death and hell, of resurrection, of great loves and great trials, of usurpation and revenge. On another level, however, it is a comedy . . . about the extreme difficulty of any dialogue between heaven and earth, about the misunderstandings that result from the 'incommensurability of things human and divine.' "[2] Each of the first three acts presents variations on the theme of self-sacrifice as an expression of love; and the levels of love and self-sacrifice are worked out in an ascending order to culminate finally in an epiphany and mystical union in Act III.

The vision is mystical in its portrayal of the union of Alcestis and Apollo in divine love; but it is existential in its illustration of the necessity of complete commitment to life in human love and self-sacrifice as the first step towards divine grace. This existentialist theme is the "lesson" that Apollo tells Death he wants to teach. The theological picture is that of a God-Creator not entirely in control of the human life he has set in motion because he has given men freedom. Not understandable to men, he tries to find means of communicating with them; but, the more he tries, the more he torments them. Death says to Apollo in Act I: "Leave these human beings alone. . . . They will never understand your language—how can they? The more you try to say something, the more you drive them distraught." Because men have freedom, they suffer the torment of living in a world in which the gods give them no aid, in which they are subject to the forces of chance and necessity, and in which their lives are without meaning except insofar as they give them meaning.

In each of the first three acts Alcestis makes a commitment to love which appears to have no value beyond itself. The greater her suffering and the more complete her commitment, the more absurdly meaningless they seem to be from the standpoint of her own welfare. But her purely human, moral commitments are indispensable first steps to the divine: they must be made without hope of reward. The young Alcestis of Act I refuses to marry Admetus because she wants to live "in the real" by devoting her life to God; any woman, she maintains, can have a family, devote her life to it, and finally sink into the grave "*loved* and *honored* but as ignorant as the day one was born" of ". . . why we live and why we die—of why the hundred thousand live and die. . . ." She wants a "sign" from Apollo that he exists and that life has a meaning. "It is time we asked for certainties," she tells her maidservant Aglaia; but just when she is ready to leave Pherai to serve Apollo at Delphi, the prophet Teiresias arrives and announces that Apollo has been commanded by Zeus to live among men for a year. Apollo has chosen Admetus' kingdom, Teiresias declares, and comes as one of four herdsmen who are waiting outside the city gates. Alcestis' first reaction is that of hope; but disillusionment with the possibility of a direct sign from Apollo comes when she sees that the "divine Teiresias" is now vulgar, mean, bitter; he is condemned like the Wandering Jew to live without hope of death.

Her disappointment in the blind prophet is followed by loss of hope from a "sign" from the drunken and dirty herdsmen who—though individually endowed with remarkable powers of cure, poetry, and vision—lack the moral consciousness that signifies divinity. Alcestis' despair at her discovery contains a hint of atheistic existentialism: "Then we are indeed miserable. Not only because we have had no aid, but we are cheated with the hope that we might have aid . . ." Her naive hopes for "certainties" shattered, she turns to a commitment of her "whole self" in love for Admetus. The first stage of her pilgrimage is, therefore, to turn away from asceticism and renunciation to "engagement" in life itself and to the creation of her own meaningful, moral existence. Her vow to live her life for Admetus comprises choosing a situation for herself: She now exists in the life of another, who likewise depends upon her for his existence. In telling Admetus she will live for him as though at any moment she might have to die for him, she unconsciously affirms her moral freedom—she is free of the bondage of trying to live according to preconceived notions about the will of God.

In Act II she puts her moral freedom to its highest test. Told that Admetus has been wounded accidentally by one of the herdsmen and must die unless someone will die for him, she decides to give her life to save him. As in Act I, her commitment is unqualified and is a "work of love"; for she insists that her sacrifice be made without consideration of self. When the herdsman who has wounded Admetus begs her to let him make the sacrifice and thus expiate his sin, she refuses to allow it, saying ". . . you would do it imperfectly; Admetus will be completely well only if I can completely die for him, give all myself to death. You wish to die, yes— but not for love of Admetus. You wish to die in order to lift the burden of that crime from off your heart." Commitment to death represents, therefore, the second step in her pilgrimage.

In Act III the scope of the action broadens to show the universal effects of Alcestis' commitments. Thessaly becomes a microcosm; its people, Mankind. A plague has gripped the city, and its citizens are in despair. The barbaric King Agis has usurped the throne and put Admetus to death. Alcestis has been spared but reduced to servitude; and, of her children, only Epimenes, who has fled, survives. But despite Alcestis' misery and suffering she—when Epimenes and his friend

Cheriander return to Thessaly to kill Agis—dissuades them and turns their efforts to helping rid the city of the plague. In spite of her losses, she also tries to give courage to Agis, whose daughter Laodarnia has just died, by convincing him life has other values besides love. "Love is not the meaning," she tells him. "It is only one of the signs that there *is* a meaning. It is only *one* of the signs that there is a meaning." While she does not spell out the other "signs," her act of kindness towards her malefactor Agis and her acceptance of responsibility for ridding Thessaly of the plague demonstrate what she means.

In existentialist terminology, Alcestis becomes a kind of spiritual legislator for mankind. Like Orestes in Sartre's *The Flies*, she is an exile in her own land; like all human beings, she is alone in the universe; and she is, therefore, at once free and responsible. But unlike Sartre's atheistic view of Orestes who becomes human in his defiance of the gods and acceptance of the burden of his people's sins, Wilder's Alcestis becomes both human and divine through finding and realizing herself in others. By turning Epimemes and Cheriander from assassination to constructive effort, she in effect unites her people against the common enemy and conquers it. In the epiphany that closes Act III, Apollo affirms the final union of the human with the eternal and the transcendent—the mystical fusion of the human soul with the principle of Life or with God or Light.

The existentialist, mystical nature of the ethical, religious, and metaphysical themes that culminate in the epiphany in Act III is unmistakable. By her actions Alcestis puts the eternal love of God into being in time through her own existence (and therefore in the lives of all who experience her act); and she achieves the paradoxical truth of the absurd: the eternal exists in the temporal, a condition which Kierkegaard conceived to be the basis of Christian faith. Alcestis' spiritual union with Apollo at her death represents the final achievement of her "eternal self." In the terminology of Kierkegaard, her pilgrimage is the process of "becoming." She becomes what she does: Giving herself completely to acts of love, sacrifice, and mercy, she becomes the incarnation of those qualities and thus establishes communication with Apollo.

Considered metaphysically, Alcestis' sacrifices have the effect of defeating the forces of chance and necessity which govern the universe. This theme is stated in the satyr-play, "The Drunken Sisters," where Apollo tricks the three Fates—Atropos, Clotho, and Lachesis—into sparing Admetus but learns that, while he can outwit them, he cannot control them. If Admetus is to live, Lachesis tells Apollo, someone else must sacrifice his life with freedom of choice: "Over such deaths we have no control. Neither Chance nor Necessity rules the free offering of the will."[3]

In the process of "becoming," Alcestis has the help of Apollo. In Act III Apollo tells Death, "I am finding that language which is received as a secret in the heart of each one, and yet which is addressed to the billions." He has also helped Admetus to yoke the lion and the boar in order to win the hand of Alcestis. And he helps Hercules bring Alcestis back from death. Preparing to descend into Hades, Hercules prays to Apollo to "Put into my arm a strength that's never been there before. You do this—or let's say: you and I do this together. And if we can do it—let everybody know that a new knowledge has been given to us of what Gods and man can do together."

Wilder's meaning in this passage bears a strong resemblance to the mystical existentialism of Nicholas Berdyaev, which holds that man participates in God's creativity and that the moral act is one of co-creation which leads ultimately to mystical union of the human and the divine. Alcestis' triumph over necessity and chance, over the injustice of Agis, and over death itself by her acts of love, sacrifice, and mercy parallels in a general way the theological precepts of Berdyaev, who maintains in his *Dream and Reality* that each moral act of love, mercy, and sacrifice helps to bring an end to the power of hatred, cruelty, and selfishness in the world. Every moral act, Berdyaev holds, concurrently diminishes necessity, enslavement, and inertia; and it brings to actual existence "a new 'other' world, where God's power is revealed in freedom and love."[4]

Although there is no extrinsic evidence that Wilder was influenced by Berdyaev, it is not unlikely that he was because the mystical nature of Berdyaev's existentialism effects the identification of the religious life with ethics and the divine in the human which Wilder tries to establish in this play. The act of co-creation by Alcestis and Apollo is a change in the order of things in which Alcestis' moral actions are expressions of God's will: they bring the promise of a "new, 'other' world." In Act I, Apollo announces the change when he says to Death: "You live in the dark and you cannot see that all things change." That the change, the victory over Death in Act II, is partly the result of Apollo's efforts is indicated in their dialogue in Act III, where Death says to Apollo in reference to Alcestis' resurrection: "You broke the ancient law and order of the world. The law—since men were created and Hell was established—that law that the living are the living and the dead are the dead." And, finally, the theme that a new, religious-moral meaning has come into the world is expressed by Apollo when he says to Death: "You are one of the few that can understand that when I talk to *one* [Alcestis], I am also talking to the innumerable."

The Alcestiad thus has a religious existentialist theme. Yet one feels while reading the play that its meaning is too often revealed by characters who are too consciously philosophical. Direct expression of ideas and interpretation of action not only render it didactic at times but preclude full realization of its potential of dramatic power. Because the action is overburdened with ideas, the plays needs in the first two acts a strong human conflict. Cocteau and Sartre brought fresh meaning to the myths they used largely because they transformed the just Greek gods into tormenters and tyrants under whom human beings suffer or rebel against—or both. Wilder's play, following generally the Greek pattern of the protagonist's departure from and gradual reconciliation with a god of wisdom, is more conventional and carries, therefore, less force and conviction. Absence of conflict also makes Alcestis' victory in Act III less impressive than it might be because it is won with less struggle than it seemingly requires. She suffers no real soul-searching before committing herself to her choices. Her dark night of the soul in Act I is brief, and no real doubts disturb her decision to turn away from Apollo and live solely for Admetus. Because of these factors, she lacks the depth and complexity a greater struggle might have given her.

The mystical nature of the theme is, however, responsible for the absence of conflict; for the tendency of mysticism to resolve conflict through love renders conflict avoidable—and desirably so. Thus Alcestis, the mystic, discourages Epimenes and Cheriander from their plan of violence against Agis and directs their efforts to helping rid Thessaly of the plague. Thus, too, the struggle over the sacrifice in Act II is not a struggle over *whether* to die for Admetus (as the argument between Pheres and Admetus in *Alcestis* is, by contrast) but over *who* will do it—Aglaia, the Herdsman, or Alcestis; and, although Alcestis decides she will do it because she most loves life and, therefore, will be making the greatest sacrifice, the fact that it *is* a great sacrifice to her is not evidenced by any visible suffering on her part. The power of love is so great that no agonizing struggle is necessary for such a sacrifice as Alcestis makes. This is what these actions imply. There is little conflict among the characters, therefore, until the last act; and even then Alcestis succeeds in preventing violence.

If one conceives of drama as an imitation of actions involving conflicts between strong protagonists, *The Alcestiad* undoubtedly is weak; for the conflicts are among characters attempting to impose value and meaning upon their lives through devotion to and sacrifice for others. The real source of conflict lies in the dialectical tension between faith and the facts of life. From the beginnning suspense is built around the questions of how Apollo and Alcestis will bridge the great gulf between the human and the divine, and of how Death—the darkest, most compelling fact of life—will be conquered. As in *The Bridge*, the facts do not justify faith. Alcestis' reward for her sacrifice appears to be the wretchedness of slavery; his labors, Hercules complains to Admetus, do not seem to justify any belief in his own divinity; and the four herdsmen, though endowed with such powers as those of the healer and the poet, do not appear to have the moral qualities requisite to divinity—or even to human dignity.

Yet all have the divine within them—and the potential to realize it, as Alcestis does in her acts of love, self-sacrifice, and mercy. Typically, Wilder puts the burden of courage and faith upon the individual as he faces the unpleasant facts of life. As the Watchman says: "The facts remain the same . . .

It is ourselves that change . . . we pray to the gods not to alter the circumstances of life but to give us the condition wherein to view them." Alcestis attains this "condition"; and, if one could wish that she had come by it and sustained it with more difficulty, he must recall that Wilder's intention is not to make the circumstances of life appear too formidable. His intention—in which he succeeds—is to show also that it is within the power of every individual to rise above despair through his exercising the great moral and ethical principles of love, self-sacrifice, justice, and mercy—and his gaining thereby the help of the gods.

Alcestis becomes, therefore, a symbol of what all men can do and be. Though she lacks complexity, she develops as few of Wilder's dramatic characters do. Her development is towards an inner serenity and moral strength which give her the will to carry on in the face of adversity and which provide her with the basis for a sound faith. From a naive belief that the "real" can be found in renunciation of life, she achieves the realization that reality is an inner thing and that the first place to look for God is within herself. Although she is one of Wilder's finest characters from the standpoint of development and growth, Alcestis' main weakness is that of the play as a whole: She conforms too much to the idea of the mystic. Moreover, because she confronts loss of faith, death, and injustice with love, sacrifice, and mercy, she becomes sentimentalized at times and seems to make her sacrifices with too much self-conscious martyrdom.

The Alcestiad is Wilder's latest major production. He was working in 1960 on a series of one-act plays for an arena theatre; and it is possible that, employing more recalcitrant and less intrinsically affirmative materials than those of *The Alcestiad*, he will utilize the devices of indirection, particularly irony, more extensively than he did in this play. A great ironist, Wilder's best work is that in which tone and themes have the self-qualifying and self-complicating qualities of irony. Should he recapture the irony of such great efforts as *Our Town* and *The Ides of March*, we can anticipate more excellent works from one of the most powerful spokesman for humanistic values of our time.

CHAPTER 6

Limitations and Achievement

IN HIS excellent "reappraisal" of Wilder in *The American Scholar* (spring, 1959), Edmund Fuller writes: "in [Wilder's] shrewd, sometimes caustic observation of *genus homo* and his history, we find one of the most searching, balanced and mature visions of ourselves as Man that any American writer offers us." In an article in the *Atlantic Monthly*, Archibald MacLeish declares: "There is no man in America . . . whose words will carry farther around the earth" than Wilder's.[1] These judgments represent, generally, the position taken by most of Wilder's admirers. They emphasize the quality of his total view of mankind and what it offers to the contemplation of the human condition and not the aesthetic qualities of his works. Critics such as Francis Fergusson who would be likely to disagree with such evaluations, might insist that, because Wilder's work is aesthetically unsatisfying, it is unsound philosophically. Viewed from outside Wilder's aesthetic and philosophical assumptions and atmosphere, the weaknesses of his art are obvious enough; and, because they are so apparent, it is perhaps well to begin a summation of his achievement by indicating what they are.

The greatest weakness of Wilder's art is that it often lacks the complexity achieved when characters and actions are presented from many viewpoints. Much of his work, built upon moral, religious, and metaphysical ideas, needs also the narrative richness that comes from having characters respond to complex social, economic, political, or psychological conditions. This lack is more apparent in his plays, which are for the most part allegorical, than in his novels; and it is more obvious in *The Woman of Andros* than in any of the other four novels. Because of his effort to give the single instance universal significance, Wilder frequently neglects to make his relation of the single instance sufficiently inclusive. Thus the melancholy of Chrysis in *The Woman* seems maudlin because the soul-deadening conventionalism which is one of her principal antagonists is not fully developed in concrete action.

Wilder's vision is most satisfyingly inclusive as a rule where his characters define themselves through objectively, or "scenically," presented conflict. The fact that *Heaven's My Destination* is a more successful novel than *The Woman of Andros* is explained by the dynamic plot of *Heaven's My Destination* in which George Brush's principles are put into action and tested by specific social obstacles which present the most formidable challenge to the traditional moral and religious values the book affirms. In this novel, moral affirmations are gained with an ironic indirection which arises by implication from the action—and not with the direct statements which characterize *The Woman*. The superiority of *The Ides of March* over *The Woman* can be explained in the same terms. In both books the conflicts are largely inner; but, while the interior monologues of Caesar either arise out of action—life as he observes it—or result in action, the inner lives of Chrysis and Pamphilus of *The Woman* consist mainly of melancholy reflections about what life means—with little in the way of dramatic incident as a basis of the reflections.

As might be expected, where the inclusiveness of a fully developed conflict is absent, Wilder achieves his moral and religious affirmations too easily. Antrobus in *The Skin of Our Teeth* survives the disasters that beset mankind, but most of mankind is destroyed by them; and we see no real suffering during his times of crisis. Granting that moral courage can help minimize the tyranny of circumstance, we do not see Antrobus' courage tested in serious conflict on the stage. Again, in *The Alcestiad* it is no real struggle for Alcestis to conquer the plague. Acting as if by impulse, she sends her son and his companion for some sulphur with which to purify the drinking water and thereby saves her people from disease. The serious problems of life, one feels while observing Alcestis solve this one, are likely to be more formidable than this. Her love and self-sacrifice would have been less efficacious if confronted with the more difficult facts of modern life—for example, the threat of annihilation by the hydrogen bomb, the problem of industrial blight, or the death struggle between giant nations holding opposed materialistic ideologies. This is not to insist, of course, that the problems of modern man cannot be dealt with in an ancient setting; for Sartre's *The Flies* is a good example of a very effective picture of man at odds with powerful social forces that deny his freedom. But where Sartre draws clearly and powerfully the antagonists to Orestes—Zeus, Aegistheus and finally Electra—Wilder fails to provide a well-defined human antagonist to Alcestis; and, with the absence of a visible struggle such as Orestes undergoes, her victory seems too easy. These are Wilder's greatest weaknesses.

The best qualities of his art are present where he wrests his most convincing affirmations from a fully developed moral conflict and when they are gained through irony—through a conflict in which moral or religious skepticism appears to gain justification but is undermined by a portrayal of great human spiritual depth and nobility. His best works from this standpoint of conflict are *The Bridge, Heaven's My Destination, The Ides of March,* and *Our Town,* where death or apparent defeat place the moral affirmation in bold relief. Less satisfactory are *The Woman, The Skin of Our Teeth,* and *The Alcestiad,* in which Wilder's themes are stated directly and arbitrarily either by dialogue or, particularly in *The Alcestiad,* through non-realistic action which leaves no moral option for those who cannot accept the mystical nature of the affirmation.

When irony is present to enrich the affirmations through qualification and understatement, Wilder's vision is most compelling. Much of the tragic effect of *Our Town,* for example, consists in the fact that life in Grover's Corners is at once beautiful and banal. The simple life as lived by the archetypal George and Emily is priceless, but Wilder offers the village drunk—a frustrated musician—as evidence that life in Grover's Corners can be deadly to talented and sensitive people. In *The Bridge,* the potential banality in the theological affirmation of mystery is avoided by an ironic transformation of a religious question into a moral one which provides an optional interpretation for both believers and non-believers; in *Heaven's My Destination,* the humanistic position arises by ironic implication from the dialectical conflict between the humanitarian Brush and the materialistic society he encounters; and, finally, in *The Ides of March,* the certitude of Caesar's skepticism is ironically subverted by what he concedes to be the "possibility of mystery" in life.

Wilder's view of life is less optimistic than it has generally been considered to be; but he has incurred the charge of unwarranted optimism mainly because of those works—most notably *The Skin of Our Teeth*—in which the full force of the dark side of his vision fails to make itself perceptible. Except for *The Matchmaker,* none of his novels or full-length plays ends "happily." From *The Cabala* to *The Ides of March* and from *Our Town* to *The Alcestiad,* his works end in death for one or another of the major characters, or in grief, or in an unsuccessful attempt to make the world better. His characters typically feel the sting of defeat; and, if they do not always show their suffering as movingly as they might (as movingly, say, as Emily does in Act III of *Our Town*), it is usually because they have come, like Chrysis in *The Woman,* to "accept from the gods all things, the bright and the dark." There is, therefore, a good deal of resignation in Wilder's characters.

The saints among men are those who, like Madre Maria in *The Bridge* and like Alcestis, affirm that life has meaning and do what they can to give it significance, accept the essentially tragic nature of life, and bring hope to a suffering humanity. Committed to responsibility for easing the suffering of their fellowmen, they point the way with love, mercy, tolerance, and understanding for those who cannot help themselves or those who are in despair.

But while courageous ones like Chrysis, Madre Maria, and Alcestis are Job-like in their praise of life, despite its apparent meaninglessness, others suffer and cause suffering through insensibility. Lack of sensitivity to other human beings—particularly the failure to respond to love with love—is the greatest human cause of suffering and, therefore, the greatest source of tragedy in Wilder's world. Her mother's failure to "realize life" through consciousness of those closest to her is the cause of Emily's heartbroken imprecations in Act III of

Our Town. Cardinal Vaini and Blair in *The Cabala,* Dona
Clara and Camila Perichole in *The Bridge,* and Clodia
Pulcher in *The Ides of March* all bring spiritual devastation
because of coldness or indifference to those who love them.
With the exception of Blair and Dona Clara, these characters
are fully and convincingly developed and the full tragic impact of their insensibility is felt in the profound grief of those
who love them. Less effective are such antagonists as Sostrata
and Chremes of *The Woman,* whose preoccupation with social
convention is inadequately expressed in action, and Cain in
The Skin of Our Teeth, whose evil is shown to be caused
after all by misunderstanding.

But while Wilder is less optimistic than he is usually considered to be and while his best works offer the most intense
portrayal of human suffering, his view of life is an affirmative
one. He does not—as T. S. Eliot does, for instance—look with
despair at the human condition in the twentieth century.
On the other hand, he has no sentimental illusions about the
innate goodness of men. The Stage Manager's comment in
Our Town that "Wherever you come near the human race,
there's layers and layers of nonsense" epitomizes the consciousness of human absurdity which pervades his work. Yet
the kind of biting satire that impugns the motives of people
is absent from Wilder's attitude to life, for men are much too
complicated to be drawn from the superficial and narrow
viewpoint of satire. A satirical attitude implies either a kind
of cynicism or the detachment of intellect from sympathetic
understanding that Wilder reprehends. Burkin in *Heaven's
My Destination,* who represents just this type of attitude, is at
once a manifestation of an unintegrated personality and a
product of a society insensitive to the profound emotional
needs of a person of superior intellect and sensibility. Burkin's
intellect is destructive because, hurt by society, he has turned
his great capacity for feeling from love to hate.

Wilder's attitude towards both satire and skepticism is also
expressed in *The Cabala* when the Cardinal declares vehe-
mently to the narrator: "I could write a book better than this
ordure that your age has offered us. . . . But a Montaigne, a
Machiavelli . . . a . . . Swift, I will never be." Satire is the
tool of the skeptic: Alone, it gives a distorted view of man-

kind. Men are absurd, and their absurdity must be made part of any comprehensive vision. But a balanced, mature vision requires a full measure of human suffering as well as of absurdity; of fulfillment in love, achievement, and joy as well as of defeat and pain; and of courage, selflessness, and nobility as well as of moral cowardice, vanity, and meanness.

All of these qualities of humanity, the good and the bad, are readily identifiable in Wilder's total view of life as expressed through his characters; and Fuller's statement that Wilder's vision is one of the most "searching, balanced and mature" perceptions that any American author offers us is for that reason unquestionably a sound judgment. Wilder's approach to life has been—like Caesar's in *The Ides of March*—one of inquiry and wonder at its mystery. Caesar's questions are Wilder's: "Man—what is that? What do we know of him? His Gods, liberty, mind, love, destiny, death—what do these mean?" And as one reads Wilder, he is almost ineluctably drawn into that same feeling of awe and wonder before the mystery of life which generates Caesar's inquiries.

Because Wilder stands back and views life as a whole and not with debilitating despair or unqualified optimism but with a tentativeness that precludes straitening dogmas or doctrines, his vision is eminently mature. Courage before the unalterable circumstances of life and responsibility for alleviating the suffering of one's fellowman—these are the moral imperatives repeated in his works. They are the indispensable elements in a meaningful, fruitful, and happy life; and it is for a full, free participation in and realization of life that Wilder appeals above all else.

But what, it is pertinent to ask, is the philosophical tradition from which his view of life and the world draws intellectual authority? As Henry James said, "The great question as to a poet or a novelist is, How does he feel about life? What, in the last analysis, is his philosophy? When vigorous writers have reached maturity, we are at liberty to gather from their works some expression of a total view of the world they have been so actively observing. This is the most interesting thing their works offer us." Wilder's "total view" is that of a humanist, but, although he shares the humanistic temperament with Irving Babbitt and Paul Elmer More, he has avoided their tendencies to make humanism a dogmatic, systematic philosophy. Moreover, because he appeals for a full, free participation in life, he has confronted the logical implications of humanism more satisfactorily than Babbitt and More did. Edmund Wilson criticized Babbitt and More because they assumed "that virtue is identical with the will to refrain"; and though Wilson was perhaps severe, he was not altogether unjustified. Wilson could not find such a negative attitude in Wilder, for to him such moral and ethical virtues as love, duty, responsibility, justice, and mercy represent positive commitments to life in action and they presuppose the full response to, and development of, the passions as well as the ethical conscience. There is also less of the spirit of Calvinism in Wilder than in Babbitt and More—particularly in respect to the "lower nature," which he does not despise as they did. He agrees substantially with his Caesar that "to deny that one is an animal is to reduce oneself to half a man," and he avoids what Joseph Wood Krutch in *The Modern Temper* called the "paradox of humanism": its tendency to deplore the very life from which the art it values so highly draws its materials.

But while Wilder does not go so far in approving response to the appetites as Hemingway, who declares in effect that whatever pleases or satisfies the senses is good, he does advocate freedom from physical restraints that impoverish or bind the spirit. In this he is more in accord with the Greek doctrine of moderation than the leaders of the Humanist movement were. Furthermore, he holds that what he calls the "wandering desires" and "blind impulses" (the "flux" was More's inclusive term for them) may have a higher meaning than they appear to have and that even the trivial events of everyday life are important. As his Caesar observes, "our lives are immersed in the trivial; the significant comes to us enwrapped in multitudinous details of the trivial; the trivial has this dignity that it exists and is omnipresent." Such a view permits him to affirm that—although its dark counterpart is admitted—"there is no part of the universe that is untouched by bliss."

Unlike such other humanists as More and T. S. Eliot, Wilder has never identified himself openly with organized

religion. But Protestantism, stripped of its sectarian color-
ations, is at the heart of his mysticism. His theologian brother,
Professor Amos N. Wilder, has written extensively about the
"Reformation Principle" of freedom and responsibility,[2] a principle that is stated or implied in all of Wilder's novels and
plays. This concept holds the individual to be free to make
his own moral choices without reference to church or state
authority but with full responsibility for them in accordance
with such broad Christian moral precepts as love, humility,
mercy, and charity. The chief consequence of the principle is
that every man is his own priest and responsible for finding
and developing those moral qualities within himself.

Examples of the presence in Wilder's works of this traditional Protestant reliance upon the judgment and reason
of the individual are almost too numerous to mention, but
one notably direct statement of it is in *The Ides of March*
when Caesar says concerning the rites of the Good Goddess,
"Let each woman find out in herself her own goddess—that
should be the meaning of these rites." And it is implicit in
Wilder's comment in his foreword to *Three Plays*: "Each
individual's assertion to an absolute reality can only be inner,
very inner."

It is also not difficult to understand, in light of this principle, why Wilder has been able without self-contradiction to
incorporate into his own philosophy some of the ethical sub-
jectivism of Sartre and some of the mystical existentialism
of Kierkegaard and Berdyaev; for, aside from the fact that
they are all humanists, these thinkers hold in common the principle of the individual's responsibility for his moral choice. But
Wilder himself is not, strictly speaking, a religious existentialist
—at least in the Kierkegaardian sense—because among other
things he does not go so far as most existentialists in emphasizing the irrational and the subjective to the exclusion of
objective knowledge. He eludes religious and philosophical
labels, but his infusion of the religious life into his moral
affirmations and his insistence upon the full development
of all the potentials of the human spirit through human relationships engendered by love and governed by reason indicates that the basis of his philosophy is personalism.

Personalism is a humanistically grounded system of assumptions that cuts through sectarian and denominational religious barriers and consolidates the intellectual forces of traditional idealism in opposition to philosophical naturalism. Considered in the light of personalism, the seemingly disparate and incompatible Platonic and existentialist, mystical and skeptical ingredients of Wilder's total vision of life can be explained as facets of a unified, coherent theory. Metaphysically, personalism restores man to his place at the center of the universe, where nineteenth-century science had replaced him with matter and force; and it holds that the mental life of man is analogous to the nature of God and that, according to Berdyaev—whose ideas have a good deal of personalism in them—the primary law of being is the person's "movement toward God, who is his ultimate end and the ultimate good of the entire universe."³

Ethically and politically, personalism distinguishes between the "person" and the "individual" in the emphasis it places upon the person as part of a community. Avoiding the extremes of the unchecked ego of individualism and the freedom-destroying statism of collectivism, it postulates the person as a unique, complex being striving for spiritual freedom and trying to create values. Rejecting in particular the Marxist economic theory of history, personalism conceives of civilization as what Emmanuel Mounier, editor of the personalist periodical *Esprit*, has called a "metaphysical response to a metaphysical call";⁴ specifically, to man's recognition of a human destiny that transcends contemporary political or economic demands.

According to J. B. Coates, Mounier "follows the existentialists in holding that human destiny is marked by anguish" and an "inescapable element of tragedy" and that the "full realization of the potentialities of the person depends upon a capacity for embracing sacrifice, risk, insecurity, and pain." But Mounier rejects "those excesses of certain existentialists who represent life as the plunge of the hopeless into nothingness"; for to him, "if life is anguish, it is also 'radiance and super-abundance, hope and love.'"⁵ This statement very nearly summarizes Wilder's view of life in its most general terms. There is nothing startlingly new in it; but personalists, borrowing freely from the idealistic tradition in carrying on the ancient battle against materialism, lay no claim to originality.

Personalism adds both social and religious dimensions to Wilder's humanism. Paralleling twentieth-century humanism in its appeal to the great tradition of literature and philosophy as at once the proof of man's higher nature and his chief source of moral and ethical authority, personalism goes beyond humanism by providing a positive social and religious purpose for the ethical will and by avoiding the "five-foot shelf" dangers T. S. Eliot objected to in humanism's narrow dependence upon the "great books" for ethical guidance and purpose. Personalism holds that the person, as a responsible member of the human community, sees his own spiritual life objectified in a purposeful relationship with others.

The theistic personalist conceives of God as the Supreme Person toward Whom men aspire in their efforts to become whole, integrated persons. "Fluid and open" in approach, as Mounier has described it, personalism is at once eclectic and undogmatic. It draws upon diverse philosophical sources but it rejects the bondage of systematic philosophy and maintains with the existentialists that the essentially subjective creation of ethical concepts in response to particular conditions precludes imposition of a system of ideas from without. This attitude, along with the humanistic aversion to absolutes, explains the absence of social doctrine in Wilder's works. It also explains his tendency not only to put his characters under conditions in which the moral choice is paramount but also to avoid the topical aspects of specific social conditions which by implication are merely current manifestations of such supratemporal forces as Chance and Necessity. For example the depression receives little attention in *Heaven's My Destination;* the unhappy people Brush meets are miserable not because they have been overwhelmed by social and economic forces but because they, in their failure to draw themselves up either morally or intellectually—or both—have made themselves victims of outside forces. Thus, too, Chance and Necessity—the social as well as the natural forces that act upon men—are conquered by Alcestis' acts of free will in love.

The effectiveness with which such a position is revealed in

a literary work depends largely upon how concretely and convincingly drawn are these formidable abstract forces—or upon how sharply etched is the discrepancy between the full realization of the powers of the human will in love and reason on one hand and the loss of consciousness and freedom in absorption with such things as custom, habit, convention, or material gain on the other. Wilder's best works from this standpoint are, again, *The Bridge, Heaven's My Destination,* and *The Ides of March* among the novels, *Our Town* among the plays; less satisfactory are *The Woman of Andros, The Skin of Our Teeth,* and *The Alcestiad.*

Wilder's characters are all personalistically conceived, for they either move towards the God within themselves in love and reason or they fail to realize their own full potential as persons. Only one—Alcestis—fully realizes the paradoxical finding and losing of self in her mystical pilgrimage; but Chrysis and Pamphilus of *The Woman of Andros* are both moving towards realization in their commitment to the life of love and reason. Ironically, Wilder's best works are those in which failure plays the biggest part. Emily's touching speech to her mother in Act III of *Our Town* reflects the failure of the people of Grover's Corners to realize all of life's potential. The great spiritual reserves of the women in *The Ides of March* are dissipated to Caesar's regret in absurd ritual; but Caesar, drawing fully upon his own passion for knowledge and putting its entire force into action, is the most powerful man in the world. In *The Cabala,* Cardinal Vaini loses his humanity as he moves away from a purposeful relationship with people (such as he once had in China) and into the spiritually insulated life of the College of Cardinals, while Astree-Luce exemplifies "the futility of goodness without intelligence." These extremes can be explained in purely humanistic terms as the unsuccessful integration of the intellect with the moral sense; but that is precisely the point: To Wilder, and to the personalist, one must become a human being—a "person"—before he can realize his own divinity. As is readily apparent, personalism is very broad and loose in its propositions. Yet it does offer religious humanists powerful intellectual weapons with which to affirm the great potential of man.

Is there any literary precedent for Wilder's personalism? As far as Walt Whitman's exuberance and stylistic super-abundance appear to be from the self-restraint and stylistic economy of Thornton Wilder, Whitman is Wilder's American literary and philosophical ancestor. Well before personalism came to be a self-conscious intellectual movement in the early years of this century, Whitman wrote in his "Democratic Vistas": ". . . what does civilization itself rest upon—and what object has it, what its religion, arts, schools, etc., but rich, luxuriant, varied personalism?" Self-reliance; identity of the individual; the nursing of idiosyncracies which save him from conformity and enable him to define and realize his purpose according to his nature; full development of the mental and physical powers, of conscience and the religious sense (without churches); full political participation without commitment to party; and the highest realization of the intrinsic qualities and dignity of womanhood—these were some of Whitman's general proposals for the perfection of individual persons and of American democracy. Like Wilder, Whitman maintained that the ideas literature conveys provide its primary justification and purpose. "The culmination and fruit of literary artistic expression," Whitman wrote in a footnote to "Democratic Vistas," "and its final fields of pleasure for the human soul, are in metaphysics, including the mysteries of the spiritual world, the soul itself, and the question of the immortal continuation of our identity."

From the bedside of the dying Catullus, Caesar, in *The Ides of March*, writes: "I am no stranger to deathbeds. To those in pain one talks about themselves; to those of clear mind one praises the world that they are quitting. There is no dignity in leaving a despicable world and the dying are often fearful lest life was not worth the efforts it had cost them. I am never short of subjects to praise." Like Whitman and in accordance with the personalist outlook, Wilder has above all else affirmed the dignity of man and the priceless value of life. He has never been short of subjects to praise.

Unlike most major writers of his time he has not pointed, therefore, to the meanness, pettiness, and animalism of man. There are no Apeneck Sweeneys, Popeyes, Congo Jakes, or Babbitts in his world. Perhaps that is a weakness in his fiction and drama. The purport of much of the criticism leveled against him indicates that many critics feel it is. But if he does not give us people whose motives are fundamentally evil or those brutalized by mechanization or enslaved by environmental and hereditary forces they cannot contend with, it is not because he denies that perdition exists in the twentieth-century world. It is because he believes that, instead of pointing to evil with scorn or horror, men must confront it with courage and wisdom.

Wilder has always maintained that no attitude or doctrine which debases the human individual by pointing to his depravity or to his helplessness can lead men to salvation. If men are insensitive, cruel, and animalistic and if they are brutalized or driven to despair by necessity or circumstance, it is the responsibility of those of cultivated sensibility and intelligence to bring the force of wisdom and courage to bear upon the suffering that results—to show the way in understanding and sympathy, as do Madre Maria, Chrysis, Caesar, Alcestis, and even George Brush, who is working his way towards that wisdom. There is little men can do to eliminate evil and circumstance, for Antrobus in *The Skin of Our Teeth* conquers neither Cain nor the natural forces that beset mankind; but they can reduce with moral courage and faith the power of those forces, keep the spark of humanity alive in the world, and carve out for themselves a meaningful and happy existence.

In an article on James Joyce (*Poetry*, March, 1941), Wilder wrote: "The price that must be paid for a love that cannot integrate its hate is sentimentality; the price that must be paid for a hate that cannot integrate its love is, variously, empty rhetoric, insecurity of taste, and the sterile refinements of an intellect bent on destruction." Wilder himself has occasionally paid the price of sentimentality. But he has never been guilty of empty rhetoric, insecurity of taste, or intellectual destructiveness; and this accomplishment is both unusual and praiseworthy in a literary era in which it is fashionable to be esoteric or iconoclastic, in which a dim view of humanity is virtually a dogma, and in which a writer supposedly lacks depth unless he is in despair.

Wilder's view is a mature one, as Fuller says, because it is the product of a balanced personality whose love and hate have been successfully integrated. He has accepted the moral responsibilities of the humanist; and, because he has consistently affirmed the dignity and worth not only of the individual person but also of American democracy, he has become, as MacLeish pointed out, perhaps the most powerful living American spokesman for the humanistic values his country was founded upon. To admit that America has largely forgotten those values does not deny the validity of them or the merit of trying to restore them in the nation's conscience and, by implication, to the hearts and minds of men everywhere. Wilder, unlike such of his contemporaries as T. S. Eliot, has written of and for the millions; and while at times— as in *The Skin of Our Teeth*—he has admittedly descended into bathos and didacticism, he has also given fresh expression to the best and most enduring values of man. It is likely, therefore, that, even though his works are less esoteric than some critics would like them to be, they will continue to bring enjoyment and intellectual stimulation to large audiences of readers and viewers long after many of our more esoteric and topical contemporary novels and plays have died quietly on library shelves.

Notes and References

Preface

1. "Why Is a Best-Seller?" *Outlook*, CXLVIII (April 18, 1928) 643.
2. Adcock, "Thornton Wilder," *The Bookman*, LXXV (March, 1929), 316-19.
3. "Thornton Wilder to the Front," *Literary Digest* (April 21, 1928), 25-26.
4. Quoted by Salpeter, *Outlook*, 634.
5. Hazlitt, "Communist Criticism," CXXXI (Nov. 26, 1930), 583-84.
6. Wilson, "The Economic Interpretation of Wilder," LXV (Nov. 26, 1930), 31-32. (Unsigned article later published in *The Shores of Light*.)
7. Cowley, *Exile's Return* (New York: The Viking Press, 1951), 304.

Chapter One

1. "An Obliging Man," *Time*, LXI (Jan. 12, 1953), 45.
2. See Malcolm Cowley's *Exile's Return* for a full treatment of the "Lost Generation" and the reasons for their self-imposed isolation.
3. More, *On Being Human* (Princeton: Princeton University Press, 1928) III, New Shelburne Essays.
4. From *Selected Essays: 1917-1932* by T. S. Eliot, copyright, 1932, by Harcourt, Brace and Company, Inc., 1932; renewed, 1960, by T. S. Eliot. Reprinted by permission of the publishers.
5. More, *On Being Human*, pp. 19-20.

Chapter Two

1. "Thornton Wilder," *Literary Chronicle: 1920-1950*, 103.
2. *Ibid.*
3. Quoted by Parmenter, "Novelist into Playwright," *Saturday Review of Literature* (June 11, 1938), 10-11.
4. Quoted by Walther Tritsch, "Thornton Wilder in Berlin," *The Living Age*, CCCXLIX (Sept., 1931), 46.

5. See *A Grammar of Motives*, (New York: Prentice-Hall, Inc., 1952). The terms "extrinsic motivations" and "intrinsic motivations" are borrowed from Mr. Burke and are used as nearly as possible in the same sense he uses them.

6. See Walther Fischer, *"The Bridge of San Luis Rey* und Prosper Merimee's *La Carosse Du Saint-Sacrement," Anglia—Zeitschrift für Englische Philologie*, Band LX, Heft 1/2 (Jan., 1936).

7. See Bruce Harkness, "The Epigraph in Conrad's *Chance," Nineteenth Century Fiction*, IX (Dec., 1954), 209-22.

8. Kenneth Burke and Stanley Remaine Hopper, "Mysticism as a Solution to the Poet's Dilemma," *Spiritual Problems in Contemporary Literature* (New York: Harper and Brothers, 1952), 105.

9. Parmenter, "Novelist into Playwright," 11.

Chapter Three

1. Tritsch, "Thornton Wilder in Berlin," *The Living Age*, CCCXLIX (Sept., 1931), 47.

2. Introduction to *Three Plays* (New York: Harper and Brothers, 1957), xii.

3. Gassner, *Form and Idea in Modern Theatre*, (New York: Holt, Rinehart and Winston, 1956), pp. 141-42. Gassner says: "The fundamental premise of realism is the Aristotelian one that drama is an imitation of an action; realists held, therefore, that the most desirable theatre is that in which imitation is closest. The fundamental premise of theatricalism is that theatre is not imitation in the narrow sense, which Aristotle never could have held, since the Greek drama upon which he based conclusions in his *Poetics* was not realistically imitative. For the theatricalist, the object of action and of all other 'imitative' elements is not imitation but *creativeness*, and a special kind of creativeness at that. The realists would agree, of course, as to the value of creativeness. But the theatricalist goes one step further, and that step is the truly decisive one for the theory and practice of pure theatricalism. He maintains that there is never any sense in pretending that one is not in the theatre; that no amount of make-believe is reality itself; that in short, theatre is the medium of dramatic art, and the effectiveness in art consists in *using* the medium rather than concealing it."

4. Introduction to *Three Plays*, xi.

5. Tritsch, 47.

6. Parmenter, "Novelist into Playwright," 10-11.

7. See Dayton Kohler, "Thornton Wilder," *English Journal,* XXVII (Jan., 1939), 6.

Chapter Four

1. See esp. Wilder's introduction to *Geographical History of America* by Gertrude Stein (New York: Random House, 1936).
2. See "An Obliging Man," *Time* (Jan. 12, 1953), 46.
3. Introduction to *Geographical History of America,* 13.
4. (Princeton: Princeton University Press, 1941.)
5. Introduction to *Geographical History of America,* 21.
6. See "Three Allegorists: Brecht, Wilder and Eliot," in Fergusson's *The Human Image in Dramatic Literature* (New York: Doubleday Anchor Books, 1957), 41-71.
7. Brown, "Wilder: *Our Town,*" *Saturday Review of Literature* (Aug. 6, 1949), 34.
8. T. S. Eliot: *The Design of His Poetry* (New York: Charles Scribner's Sons, 1949), 101.
9. *The Nation,* CLXXVI (Dec. 4, 1955), 562.
10. See esp. "James Joyce (1888-1941)," *Poetry*: *A Magazine of Verse,* LVII (March, 1941), 370-74.
11. Part I, XXV (Dec. 19, 1942), 3.
12. See Robinson's "The Strange Case of Thornton Wilder," *Esquire,* XLVII (March, 1957), 71, 124-26.
13. See Wilson's "The Antrobuses and the Earwickers," *The Nation,* CLVI (Jan. 30, 1943), 167-68.
14. "The Skin of Whose Teeth?" Part II, *Saturday Review of Literature* (Dec. 26, 1942), 11.
15. *Time,* XL (Dec. 28, 1942), 62.
16. Cf. Wilson's "The Antrobuses and the Earwickers" (note 13 above) for the most convincing expression of this view.
17. See Gassner's *Form and Idea in Modern Theatre,* p. 143. Gassner maintains that *Skin* is the best theatricalist play in American theatre, except for Cummings' dadaist-surrealist play *him.*

Chapter Five

1. "Existentialism and Humanism," translated with an Introduction by Philip Mairet (London: Mathuen and Company, Ltd., 1949). (French ed. first published in 1946.)
2. Quoted by Paul M. Cubeta, *Modern Drama for Analysis* (New York: Holt, Rinehart and Winston, Inc., 1955), 595-96.
3. Quoted from Berdyaev's *Dream and Reality* by F. H. Heineman in *Existentialism and the Modern Temper* (New York: Harper and Brothers, 1958), 161.

Chapter Six

1. MacLeish, "The Isolation of the American Artist," *The Atlantic Monthly*, CCI (Jan., 1958), 59.

2. See esp. *Spiritual Aspects of the New Poetry* (New York: Harper and Brothers, 1940).

3. Quoted by J. B. Coates in *The Crisis of the Human Person* (*Some Personalist Interpretations*), (New York: Longmans, Green and Co., 1949), 12.

4. *Ibid.*, 17-18.

Selected Bibliography

WORKS PUBLISHED BY THORNTON WILDER

The Trumpet Shall Sound. In *Yale Literary Magazine* (Oct., 1919 to Jan., 1920 inclusive).

"A Diary: First and Last Entry," *S4N* (Feb., 1924).

The Cabala. New York: Albert and Charles Boni, Inc., 1926.

The Bridge of San Luis Rey. New York: Albert and Charles Boni, Inc., 1927.

The Angel That Troubled the Waters. New York: Coward-Mc-Cann, Inc., 1928.

"Playgoing Nights: From a Travel Diary," *Theatre Arts Monthly,* XIII (June, 1929), 411-19. (Written in collaboration with Isabel Wilder.)

The Woman of Andros. New York: Albert and Charles Boni, Inc., 1930.

The Long Christmas Dinner and Other Plays in One Act. New York: Coward-McCann, Inc., 1931.

Heaven's My Destination. New York: Harper and Brothers, 1935.

Introduction to *Narration: Four Lectures* by Gertrude Stein. Chicago: University of Chicago Press, 1935, v-viii.

Introduction to *The Geographical History of America* by Gertrude Stein. New York: Random House, 1936.

Our Town. New York: Harper and Brothers, 1935.

Introduction to *Oedipus the King.* New York: The Heritage Press. No date given.

"James Joyce (1882-1941)," *Poetry: A Magazine of Verse,* LVII (March, 1941), 370-74.

"Some Thoughts on Playwrighting," in *The Intent of the Artist,* ed. Augusto Centeno (Princeton: Princeton University Press, 1941), 83-98.

The Skin of Our Teeth. New York: Harper and Brothers, 1942.

The Ides of March. New York: Harper and Brothers, 1948.

"World Literature and the Modern Mind," in *Goethe and the Modern Age,* ed. Arnold Bergstrasser (Chicago: Henry Regnery Company, 1949), 213-24.

"Fraternity of Man." *Time,* LVIII (July 2, 1951), 61. (Report of Wilder's Commencement Address at Harvard, June, 1951.)

"Toward an American Language." *The Atlantic Monthly,* CLXXXX (July, 1952), 29-37.

"The American Loneliness." *The Atlantic Monthly,* CLXXXX (Aug., 1952), 65-69.

"Emily Dickinson." *The Atlantic Monthly,* CLXXXX (Nov., 1952), 43-48.

"Silent Generation." *Harpers,* CCVI (April, 1953), 34-36.

The Matchmaker. New York: Harper and Brothers, 1955.

Preface to *Three Plays.* New York: Harper and Brothers, 1957.

"Kultur in einer Demokratie." S. Fischer Verlag, 1957. (Pamphlet.)

WORKS USEFUL TO THE STUDENT OF WILDER

I. Criticism of Wilder's Work:

"An Obliging Man." *Time* (Jan. 12, 1953), 44-49. Particularly valuable in showing the influence of Gertrude Stein on Wilder.

COWLEY, MALCOLM. Introduction to *A Thornton Wilder Trio.* New York: Criterion Books, Inc., 1956. This excellent article is a must for all readers of Wilder, for it relates how he differs from his contemporaries in his use of moral themes and in his historical perspective; it was also published earlier in a slightly longer form as "The Man Who Abolished Time" in *SRL* (Oct. 6, 1956), 13-14, 50-52.

FERGUSSON, FRANCIS. "Three Allegorists: Brecht, Wilder and Eliot," *The Sewanee Review,* LXIV (fall, 1956), 544-73. Reprinted in Fergusson's *The Human Image in Dramatic Literature* (New York: Doubleday Anchor Books, 1957), 41-71. Points to lack of historical dimension as major weakness of Wilder's dramatic work.

FIREBAUGH, JOSEPH. "The Humanism of Thornton Wilder," *The Pacific Spectator,* IV (autumn, 1950), 426-28. One of the best works on Wilder to date, this article defines Wilder's humanism broadly in terms of recurrent themes.

FULLER, EDMUND. "Reappraisals: Thornton Wilder: 'The Notation of the Heart,'" *The American Scholar,* XXVIII (spring, 1959), 210-17. Evaluates Wilder's achievement and places him among the great writers of our time on the basis of his complex and mature vision.

GUTHRIE, TYRONE. "The World of Thornton Wilder," *New York Times Magazine* (November 27, 1955), 26-27, 64, 66-68. A perceptive survey of Wilder's vision by a man who has directed some of Wilder's plays.

KOHLER, DAYTON. "Thornton Wilder," *English Journal,* XXVIII (Jan., 1939), 1-11. Particularly good appraisal of Wilder's style.

McNamara, Robert. "Phases of American Religion in Thornton Wilder and Willa Cather," *The Catholic World*, CXXXV (Sept., 1932), 641-49. Traces Wilder's early attempts to remind Americans of their religious heritage.

Parmenter, Ross. "Novelist into Playwright," *Saturday Review of Literature* (June 11, 1938), 10-11. Shows dramatic qualities of early novels as stages in Wilder's development as a dramatist.

Scott, Winfield Townley. "*Our Town* and the Golden Veil," *Virginia Quarterly Review*, XXIX (Jan., 1953), 103-17. Describes the dualistic nature of *Our Town*, the fusion of past and present, natural and supernatural.

Stürzl, Erwin. "Weltbild und Lebensphilosophie Thornton Wilders," *Die Neueren Sprachen*, Heft 8, 1955, 341-51. Shows relationship between Wilder's extensive travel and the universality of his themes.

Wilson, Edmund. "The Antrobuses and the Earwickers," *The Nation*, CXVI (Jan. 30, 1943), 167-68. Best appraisal of the *Skin of Our Teeth-Finnegans Wake* controversy; justifies Wilder's borrowing from Joyce.

————. "Dahlberg, Dos Passos and Wilder," "Mr. Wilder in the Middle West," "Thornton Wilder," "The Economic Interpretation of Wilder," in *The Shores of Light*. New York: Farrar, Straus and Young, 1952. Perceptive studies of Wilder's first four novels.

————. "Thornton Wilder: The Influence of Proust," *New Republic*, LV (Aug. 8, 1928), 303-5.

II. Valuable Background Sources:

Bentley, Eric. *The Playwright as Thinker*. New York: Meridian Books, 1957. A thorough treatment of "The two traditions of modern drama": realism and anti-realism.

Brightman, Edgar Sheffield. *Nature and Values*. New York: Abingdon-Cokesbury Press, 1946. An important personalist work.

Coates, J. B. *The Crisis of the Human Person (Some Personalist Interpretations)*. New York: Longmans, Green and Co., 1949. Discussions of important personalist thinkers.

Cowley, Malcolm. *Exile's Return*. New York: The Viking Press, 1951. One of the best works on the American literary exiles of the twenties—the men and women of Wilder's generation.

Fulton, A. R. "Expressionism—Twenty Years After," *Sewanee Review*, LII (summer, 1944), 210-17. Notes the expressionistic elements of *Our Town* and *The Skin of Our Teeth*.

Selected Bibliography

GASSNER, JOHN. *Form and Idea in Modern Theatre.* New York: The Dryden Press, 1956. Puts Wilder in the theatricalist tradition of dramaturgy. Indispensable to the understanding of Wilder's place in modern drama.

HOPPER, STANLEY ROMAINE. (ed.). *Spiritual Problems in Contemporary Literature.* New York: Harper and Brothers, 1952. See esp. "Mysticism as a Solution to the Poet's Dilemma" by Hopper and Kenneth Burke for insight into Wilder's resolution of the conflict between skepticism and faith.

MORE, PAUL ELMER. *On Being Human* (New Shelburne Essays, III), Princeton: Princeton University Press, 1936. The New Humanism explained by one of its leading figures.

WILDER, AMOS NIVEN. *Spiritual Aspects of the New Poetry.* New York: Harper and Brothers, 1940. The religious point of view in this book is very close to that revealed in Thornton Wilder's work.

Index